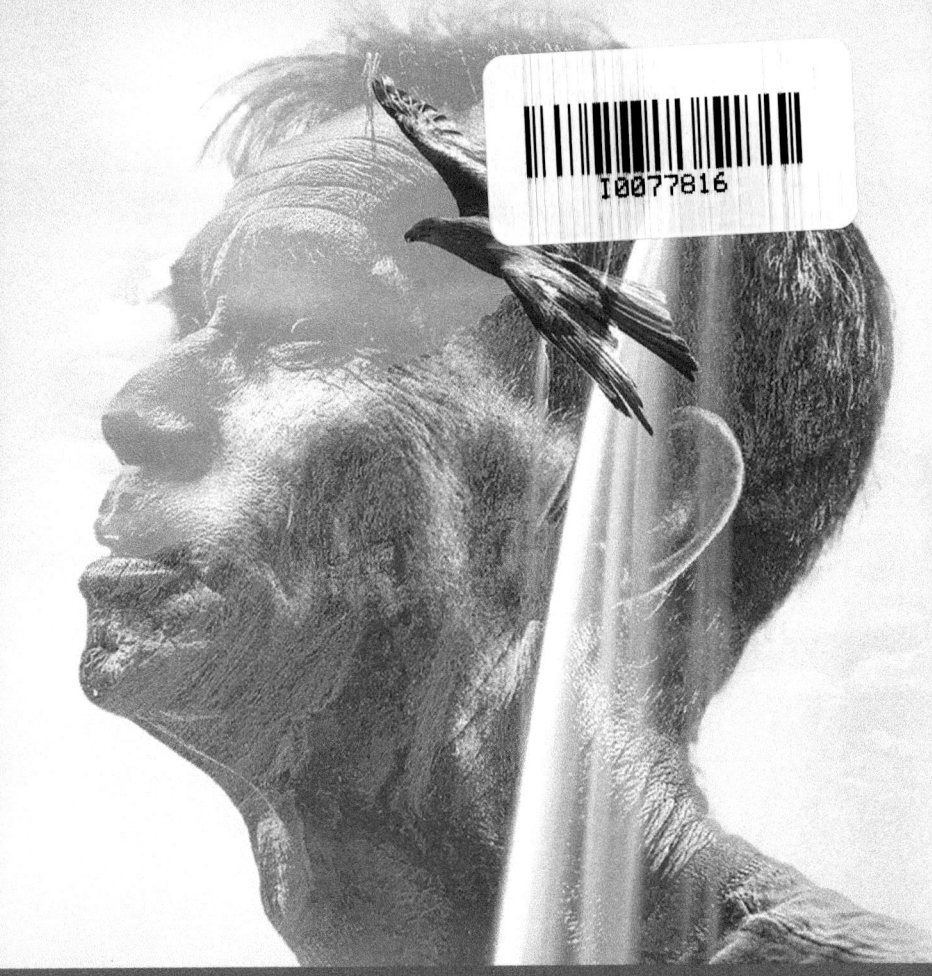

IDENTITY SERIES
CODE ONE

IDENTITY SERIES - CODE 1

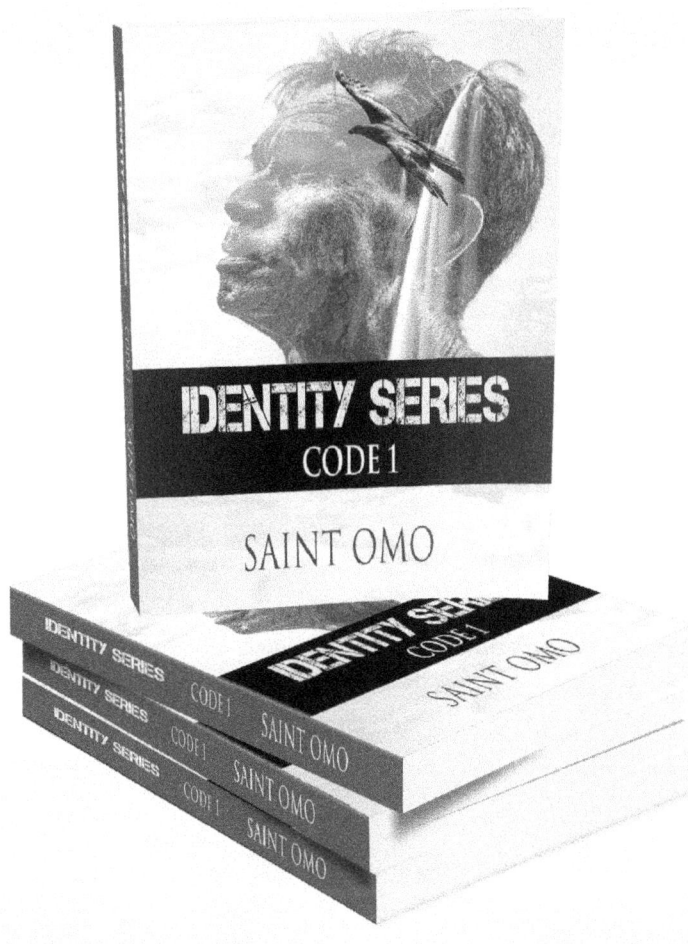

REHOBOTH HOUSE™

IDENTITY SERIES - CODE ONE

Copyright © 2019 By Saint Omo

ISBN: 978-1-64301-017-5

This book is published in the United States of America by Rehoboth House, Chicago and printed by permission in Nigeria by Rehoboth Publishing, Lagos.

The opinions expressed by the author in this book are exclusively his and not those of Rehoboth House.

All rights reserved. Reproduction of this material, in whole or part, by whatever means, without the express written consent by the author is not permitted.

Take note that the name of satan and related names are not capitalised. We choose not to acknowledge him, even to the point of violating grammatical rules.

Unless otherwise indicated, all scripture quotations are taken from the Authorized King James Version of the Holy Bible (KJV).

Author's Contact
Yahweh To Face Academy: For teachings, seminars, and workshops
Email: omoregbei62@gmail.com. or call +234 809 226 6692
facebook.com/saint.omo.5

Placing Online Order for the Book Visit
amazon.com, barnesandnoble.com, and other online bookstores.
Author's website: saintomo.com

Cover Designed by
Daniel PROTECH Designers

Interior Designed by Rehoboth House, Chicago
www.rehobothhouseonline.com
email:info@rehobothhouseonline.com

First Print, April 2019
By Rehoboth Publishing,
174 Ikorodu Road, Lagos
Tel: 234-802-304-3072
E-mail: rehobothpublishing@gmail.com

REHOBOTH HOUSE

IDENTITY SERIES - CODE 1

TABLE OF CONTENTS

Dedication..ix

Acknowledgment...xi

Foreword..xiii

Introduction...xv

MIRROR ONE:

Love...1

MIRROR TWO:

Believers Are One Spirit With the Immortal Christ................................15

MIRROR THREE:

God Has Finished His Work...33

MIRROR FOUR:

Veil..51

MIRROR FIVE:

He Is A Life-Giving Spirit..67

MIRROR SIX:

Embrace Teachings That Reveal Your Spirit's Nature............................85

MIRROR SEVEN:

Christianity Is the Fellowship Of Gods..99

MIRROR EIGHT:

He Sees Us As He Is..113

MIRROR NINE:

Redemption...131

MIRROR TEN:

Yielding Yourself...155

The Blurb 173

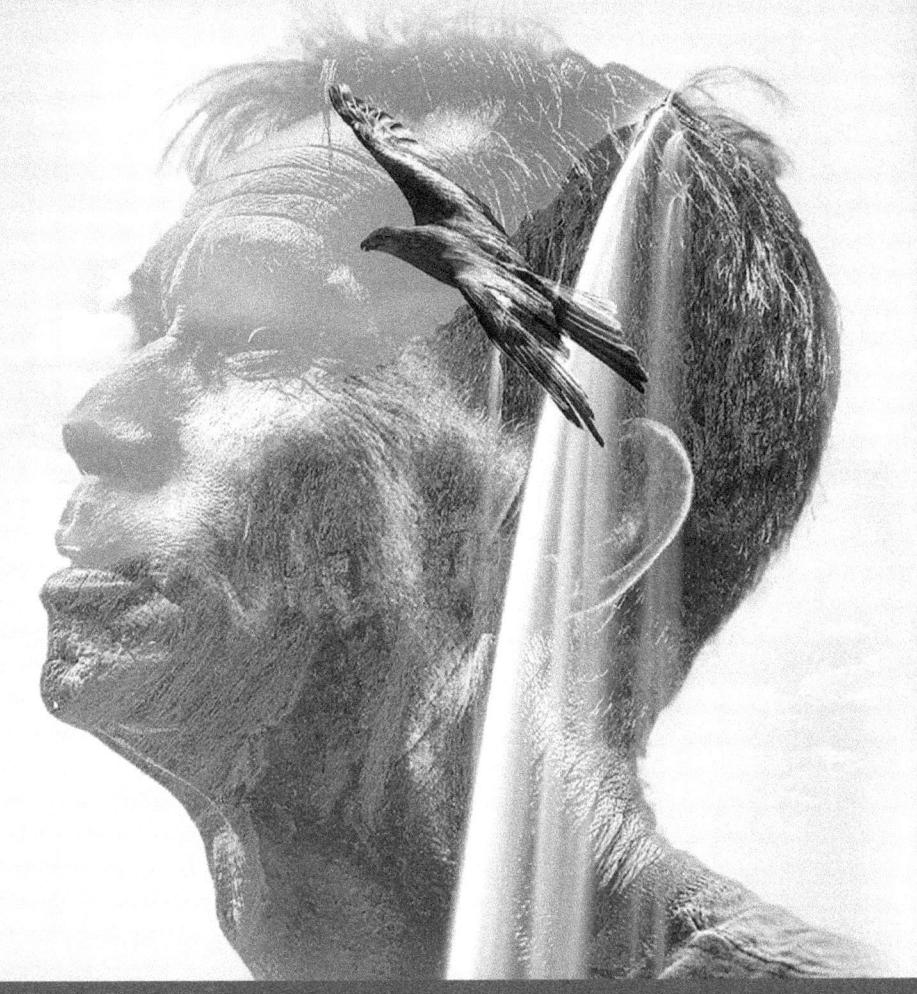

DEDICATION
IDENTITY SERIES

IDENTITY SERIES - CODE 1

DEDICATION

This book is dedicated to all seekers of TRUTH.

FOREWORD
TEACHING SERIES

IDENTITY SERIES - CODE 1

FOREWORD

The key to growth in stature is locked up in nature. Because like in every life form, the limitations and potentials of a being are encoded in the records of its DNA, which define its character. Hence the most significant revelation a person can have is the revelation of his identity, which is a revelation of his nature.

> *For the new creation, what does it really mean when the scripture says "YE are sons born of God" (John 1:12-13)?*

In simple terms, it means that to understand who the new creation is, you have to look at the Father. The Unveiling of the Father is the Revealing of The Son. But the Father was revealed in Christ who is His express image and 'we are complete in Him. Thus, Christ became the common denominator.

> *"For in him (Christ) dwelleth all the fulness of the Godhead bodily. And ye are complete in him, which is the head of all principality and power" Colossians 2:9-10 (KJV).*

My dear believers, Saint Omo, has by the spirit of the word, captured what I would like to call "Codes of the Christ Genome." The codes are inexhaustible. And many are too incredible to be true when looked at with natural eyes. But they are our eternal reality.

> *"But we all, with open face beholding as in a glass the glory of the Lord, are changed into the same image from glory to glory, even as by the Spirit of the Lord" 2 Corinthians 3:18 (KJV).*

FOREWORD

In reading this book, you will come face to face with the reality that is yours as the new creation, and in beholding that reality, you will begin to walk experientially in that which you already are.

So buckle your seat belts. It's time to fly.

Dr Oje Valentine Ikenna
Mystic Medic
Nigeria.

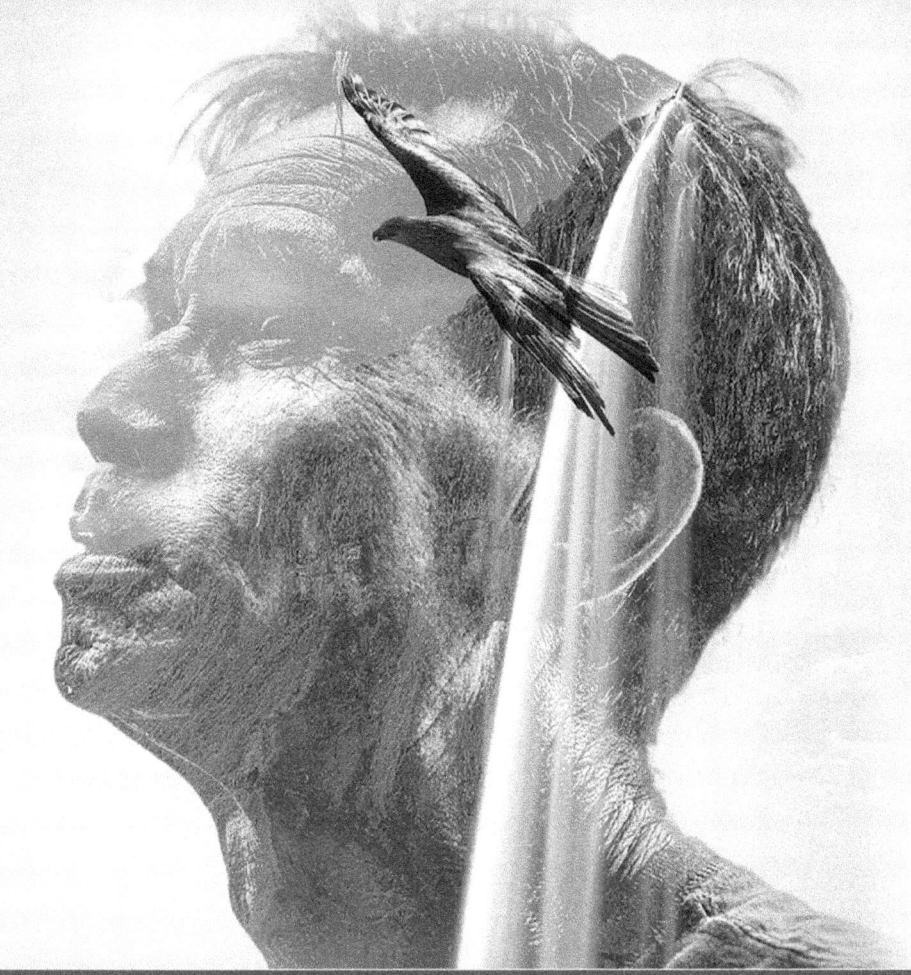

INTRODUCTION
TEACHING SERIES

IDENTITY SERIES - CODE 1

INTRODUCTION

Believers must realize that what they are supposed to be learning to manifest their true identity is clearly revealed, which is the revelation of the mystery of God who is Christ, hence the curriculum of the believer.

If the believer must know himself and manifest his spirit's nature, then he must have a clear cut understanding of the revelation knowledge of Christ. At the unveiling of Christ is the revelation of who the believer is.

This book is written in a series to show who the believer is in the light of truth revealed in Christ. Every page serves as a mirror for the believer to see himself as he is in Christ.

Keep up with the series and experience the transformation God desired for you.

You are blessed.

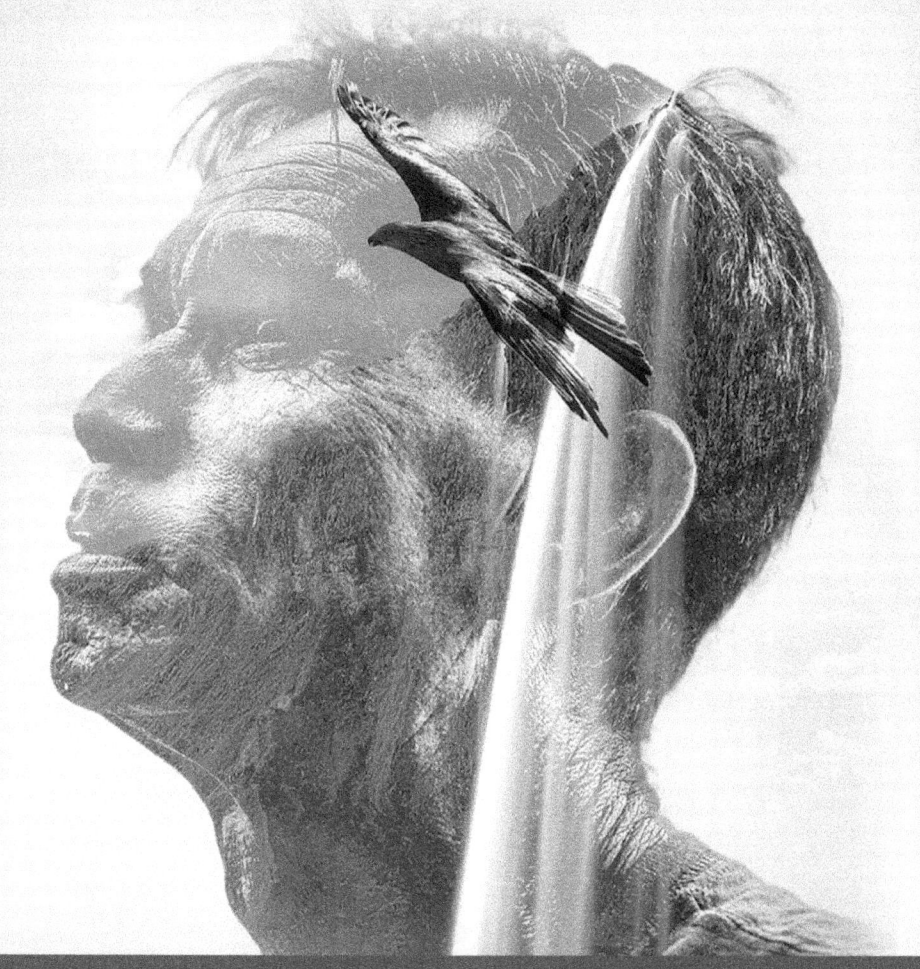

MIRROR ONE
TEACHING SERIES

IDENTITY SCHOOL OF REDEMPTION | 1

IDENTITY SERIES - CODE 1

MIRROR 1.0
Love

Love is the expression and identity of my spirit. It is the very substance of my essence. Walking in love is the outflow of my life in the spirit. It is God's river of life encapsulated in the human body for a dying and thirsty world.

- I am love
- I am life
- I am immortal
- I am a river of life
- I am righteousness
- I know who I am and where I came from.
- I release life when I speak because my words are seasoned with grace.
- I am submerging the dying and thirsty world into the very substance of my essence.

Christ is the identity of my spirit. I am whom He became at the resurrection, and He is who I am in Him.

We both coinhere each other as one eternally inseparable substance. We are one spirit.

MIRROR ONE

I am the substance of God's eternal word because I was begotten of Him by His incorruptible word that lives and abides forever. This is my conviction, my confession, and my affirmation.

MIRROR 1.1
Thoughts

Thoughts are spiritual signals that reveal the condition of the heart.

Jesus could pick up the signal of people's thought and understood the state of their heart.

> **Matthew 9:4** *"And Jesus knowing their thoughts said, Wherefore think ye evil in your hearts?"*

We may have heard that the devil doesn't know what is in our heart. This is not very true. In general, spirits can understand by the signals that our thoughts project. In some cases, spirits can discern the thoughts of our minds and know what is in our hearts. Thoughts are doorways to the heart of man.

Our thoughts are substantial and can be perceivable by spirit beings. We must watch and guard our thoughts and bring them under the control of the word of God. I believe this is the reason God gave us a prescription of what should guard our thought life.

> *"Finally, brethren, whatever things are true, whatever things are noble, whatever things are just, whatever things are pure, whatever things are lovely, whatever things are of good report, if there is any virtue and if there is anything praiseworthy—meditate on these things" Philippians 4:8 (NKJV).*

In, fact, as you pay careful attention to your thought rebuke quickly every unhealthy thought; to dwell upon them is to invite the presence of dark spirits in your life.

This is why you must always wrap your thought on the truth of your spirit's identity in the immortal Christ because in doing so you extend a hand of fellowship to unseen beings within the terrain of light.

Any thought that attempts to oppose and exalt itself against the knowledge of God must be taken captive to obey Christ.

> *"Casting down arguments and every high thing that exalts itself against the knowledge of God, bringing every thought into captivity to the obedience of Christ, and being ready to punish all disobedience when your obedience is fulfilled" 2 Corinthians 10:5-6 (NKJV).*

Unsanctified thoughts not guided and influenced by the word of God, attract the presence of demons which triggers evil either in words or actions.

Lastly, I will also like you to know that the kingdom of darkness projects certain thoughts us. We must sharply rebuke them and never accept such thought as ours.

MIRROR ONE

"The thoughts of the righteous are right, But the counsels of the wicked are deceitful" Proverbs 12:5 (NKJV).

MIRROR 1.2
The Word Of God

The word of God is the substance and nature of our spirit because we are begotten of Him. We are the offspring of the word of truth. Our spirit is truth.

"Of His own will He brought us forth by the word of truth, that we might be a kind of firstfruits of His creatures" James 1:18 (NKJV).

"Being born again, not of corruptible seed, but of incorruptible, by the word of God, which liveth and abideth forever" 1 Peter 1:23.

Dear believer, the word of God is not something coming to you from outside of you; it is actually Christ revealed from within you. The nature of your spirit is Christ. You are one substance with Him.

"But he that is joined unto the Lord is one spirit" 1 Corinthians 6:17.

Do You Know Who You Are?

We have the written word of God (the Bible), and we have the living word of God, which is the nature of our spirit in the immortal Christ. I am the living word of the father in Christ.

The written word was given to me to educate my soul concerning the nature of my new spirit in the immortal Christ. So I don't study the word to become what God's word says because I am what the written word says already in Christ. My study of the written word is an immersion of my soul in the knowledge of the identity of my spirit in the immortal Christ.

MIRROR 1.3
I Am What He Became At The Resurrection

The totality of the "in Christ realities" is this; I am what He became at the resurrection.

Dear believer, I only have one message for you, and I will forever sound the alarm. Your soul must be fully immersed in the knowledge of the identity of your spirit in the immortal Christ. You are now immortal, even though you live in an earthly tabernacle (Your Body). God is the substance of your being you are one with God now.

Understand that the nature of your spirit contains all that God is, in His uncreated estate. God sees you as Himself, and He wants you to think of yourself in the light of who He is and who you have become in the immortal Christ. I am in love with my heavenly Father.

MIRROR 1.4
What Is Pride?

What the immortal Christ considers as humility is pride to sense based knowledge people. When a dead spirit (unbeliever) says he is righteous because he has done good works, God considers him as proud, but when he says before God that he is a sinner despite the good he has done, God reckons him humble. The issue here is about the nature of the man. The truth is that as sin is a nature, so is righteousness.

The first, presented a false reality of his nature by his good works while the last stayed through to his true nature, despite his good works. But the story changes with the immortal spirits (believers) in Christ.

God considers us humble when we insist on who we are in our spirit's nature, irrespective of our works in the flesh. We must never describe ourselves based on our works but the identity of our spirit in the immortal Christ. In so doing our mind get renewed with the life of God and eventually impacts on our works.

IDENTITY SERIES - CODE 1

MIRROR 1.5
Confession

My humble confession is that I am one spirit with the immortal Christ. LORD, as you are so, am I in you."

- Christ is life
- Christ is God
- Christ is love
- Christ is immortal
- Christ is righteousness

"Herein is our love made perfect, that we may have boldness in the day of judgment: because as he is, so are we in this world" 1 John 4:17.

MIRROR 1.6
Believers Nature Is Life

Dear believer because of righteousness the nature of your spirit is life, which is now your essence in the immortal Christ. It should influence your thinking and ultimately your actions in the flesh. Know who you are in the immortal Christ.

MIRROR ONE

Consistently dwell upon the identity of the personality and nature of your spirit via meditative prayer. You are righteousness. Your soul must feed daily on this truth. This is how we break free from unsanctified imaginations and desires that seek to linger in our soul. We shrink the conduit of the soul and short-circuits the outflow of life emanating from the spirit's nature when we feed on the knowledge of sin and death. This explains why we don't make much impact as we should because the channel of the river of life that should flow from the nature of the spirit has been choked by what we feed on daily.

Dear immortal spirit (believer) open wide the channel for the outflow of life by letting your soul feed on the truth of your spirit essence in the immortal Christ.

The template for your soul is your spirit's nature. Your mind must continuously behold the identity of your spirit and be baptised into the reality of the nature of your spirit. This is how we impose the reality of the nature of our spirit on our present mortal bodies, such that even in its unglorified state it begins to experience the life and reality of the nature of our spirit in the immortal Christ.

Do you know that the nature of your spirit is ageless? If you don't know before, now you know. The aging of the body is an experience of death but glory to Jesus, my lover who has made me free from the law of sin and death by the law of the spirit of life living in my spirit.

IDENTITY SERIES - CODE 1

Once again, please dwell upon this revelation of who you are in your new nature in Christ immortal. You are loved immortal spirit.

MIRROR 1.7
The New Creation Man

At the point of the new birth experience the old nature was never improved upon, it was utterly crucified (executed) Therefore, you are now a perfect new being in Christ.

> 2 Corinthians 5:17 *"Therefore if any man be in Christ, he is a new creature: old things are passed away; behold all things are become new."*

In reality, as an immortal spirit in Christ, you are not a sinner saved by grace. Though, in retrospect, that was who you were. But now as a new creation in Christ, you have no past sins. Because you have never existed, you don't have any record of past life. The record now is that you are completely a new creation and a spotless virgin in Christ. The nature of your spirit is righteousness and have no sin.

This is why you are forever in the presence of God as a new creature in Christ. In other words, the presence of God is the natural habitat of your spirit in Christ. This is why you don't come and go out of His presence, you were born there, and you live there forever.

However, to experience the reality of this new man, you must soak your consciousness with this priceless truth. Living in this new creation reality destroys the mental servitude that has enslaved most believers and brings out the kingly dimension of the divine nature of your spirit. You are not a slave.

MIRROR 1.8
Believers Feed On The Living Word Of God

As priests of the immortal God, we function by feeding on the living word which is the knowledge of our spirit in the immortal Christ. Spirit identity-based teachings are not mere sermons and Bible head knowledge. I am not a Bible teacher who feeds the head with Bible knowledge. I am an immortal priest of the living God serving the soul with bread and wine. The mystery of the bread and wine introduced by Melchizedek in Genesis 14 captures the knowledge of the nature of our spirit in the immortal Christ.

> *"Then Melchizedek king of Salem brought out bread and wine; he was the priest of God Most High"* Genesis 14: 18 (NKJV).

All we need is an open and sincere heart in love to embrace all of God that had been worked into our spirit. I am an immortal priest with a focus. I stick to my function as one who serves the soul with bread and wine in the knowledge of the nature of our spirit in the immortal Christ.

For the hungry soul, bread and wine are currently being served to you. Eat and rejoice in the kingdom of your Father. This is my humble submission.

MIRROR 1.9
The Eternal Purpose Of God

The eternal purpose of God is to reproduced His immortal Christ. We must be persistent in soaking our consciousness in the revealed knowledge of the identity and nature of our spirit. We must never be careless with these eternal realities. The reprogramming of the soul with the revelation knowledge of the nature of our spirit in the immortal Christ requires us to be determined and spontaneous as we relate with the Spirit.

God has accomplished His eternal purpose in the immortal Christ. His purpose was to reproduce His immortal life in the spirit of the new man in Christ, which is now our new nature. This is the summation of the righteousness of God in Christ Jesus. The immortal life of God is the nature of our spirit in Christ. Our spirits' nature is the finished work of God in the immortal Christ. Therefore, we are complete in the immortal Christ.

You can't improve on the new creation man because he is "god" and perfect in nature. This new nature of the believer does not grows, the believer only grows in the revelation knowledge of

MIRROR ONE

who he is as righteousness, as he renews his soul in the revelation knowledge of the nature of his spirit in the immortal Christ. Dear believer, this is a revolution that has not yet been fully embraced by the Church. The power and glory of the immortal Christ living in our physical bodies is a reality that this generation is beginning to understand and experience in a measure that has not been before. I dare to say that it is the ultimate of revelations being released from the heart of the Father.

> *"I have said, Ye are gods; and all of you are children of the most High" Psalm 82:6.*

Jesus reemphasizes this eternal TRUTH!

> *"Jesus answered them, "Is it not written in your Law, 'I have said you are "gods"'[a]? If he called them 'gods,' to whom the word of God came—and Scripture cannot be set aside— what about the one whom the Father set apart as his very own and sent into the world? Why then do you accuse me of blasphemy because I said, 'I am God's Son'? John 10:34-36 (NIV).*

We give everything up for this and brood daily on this. It is priceless, and we embrace all of it.

MIRROR TWO
TEACHING SERIES

IDENTITY SCHOOL OF REDEMPTION

IDENTITY SERIES - CODE 1

MIRROR 2.0

Believers Are One Spirit With The Immortal Christ

We are one substance with the immortal Christ. We are in Him what He became at the resurrection. The nature of our spirit is life-giving. We are quickening spirits in the immortal Christ.

The revelation knowledge of our spirit's nature as a quickening spirit helps us to function as life givers. It helps us to know that we are self-sustaining and sufficient in the immortal Christ, just as the father has life in Himself, we also have life in ourselves in the immortal Christ.

> *"For as the Father hath life in himself; so hath he given to the Son to have life in himself" John 5:26.*

> *"For even as the Father has life in Himself and is self-existent, so He has given to the Son to have life in Himself and be self-existent" John 5:26 (AMPV).*

This doesn't mean that we are now independent of God or equal with Him. Assuredly, there is no sense of competition in the family of immortal spirits. But it does mean that God's self-existing life has completely been consummated in us, this is what it means to have His eternal life in our spirit. Our new nature is God's self-existing life in the immortal Christ.

MIRROR TWO

"For ye are dead, and your life is hid with Christ in God. When Christ, [WHO IS] OUR LIFE, shall appear, then shall ye also appear with him in glory" Colossians 3:3-4.

Again, we are self-existing does not imply that we are separate from Him. We are self-existing, self-sustaining and self-sufficient because the immortal Christ is our very life; hence, He is our existence, our sustenance, and our sufficiency, We are ONE SPIRIT with Him. I hope you got the point?

He is who we are in Him, we are what He became at the resurrection. Our spirits' nature is the immortal Christ. Love made us who we are in Him. This is why love is the very substance of our spirits' nature. Love is an immortal spirit. Walking in love is the outflow of the nature of our spirit in the immortal Christ.

Dear believer, your salvation experience was God actually given birth to Himself in you, in the immortal Christ.

Do you know who you are?

MIRROR 2.1
At New Birth God Brought Forth Himself In Christ

The nature of our spirit in the immortal Christ captures the complete knowledge (epignosis) of God in His uncreated estate. As an immortal spirit in Christ, you are all knowing. It is your soul that needs a revelation of the knowledge of God. Hence the progression in revelation knowledge is a soul-based experience.

To say we don't know is a wrong confession from an immortal spirit in Christ. Our spirit potentially has complete knowledge and details of everything both created and uncreated. Our soul has to be renewed to function in that realm. The all-knowing capacity is inherent in our spirit.

Our soul may not yet know what our spirit knows because it is on a journey of learning to arrive at the full stature of the knowledge of our spirit, which is actually the knowledge of the Son of God.

What we do is that we SEARCH OUT details of things in our spiritual nature. As we gradually train our consciousness through a consistent practice of meditation, we cultivate a posture of heart that can easily find out detail information about things.

Dear believer, understand that at the point of your new birth experience, God brought forth Himself in Christ. He didn't give birth to immortal spirits who are substandard to Himself.

To accurately define who you are, you have to look at God. He is your spirit's nature in Christ. Mental servitude is forever punished in hell because we know who we are in Him.

What He is at the resurrection is what we became in Him in our new birth experience.

MIRROR TWO

MIRROR 2.2
WHAT IS SPIRITUAL KNOWING

Accumulating biblical information is not equal to spiritual knowledge. Spiritual knowledge is having a revelation knowledge of the nature of our spirit in the immortal Christ, which helps to facilitate experiences in the soul to be aligned with the spirit.

Don't ever be satisfied with acquiring mere Bible knowledge. Go beyond it and cultivate a consistent practice of engaging your soul in the act of meditation by which spiritual knowledge and experiences are attained.

In meditation, the totality of our soul gains a posture of stillness where it can perfectly gaze into the depth of our being in its fundamental reality in the immortal Christ. This is how God writes the books of Himself already contained in our spirit's personality. Our soul is being reconfigured by beholding the Christ of our being. I will not go further on meditation, but this is to stir you up for a personal and further search.

The act of meditation is almost a lost practice in the treasured Body of Christ, most especially among the Pentecostal and Charismatic circle. Glory be to God that many are beginning to rediscover such golden well of treasure.

IDENTITY SERIES - CODE 1

MIRROR 2.3
Gaze At The Inner Glory

Dear believer, don't be concerned and troubled about many things. The Lord said, only ONE THING is needed, which is to gaze at the inner GLORY of the immortal Christ in your spirit's nature.

> "Now it happened as they went that He entered a certain village, and a certain woman named Martha welcomed Him into her house. And she had a sister called <u>Mary, who also sat at Jesus' feet and heard His word.</u> But Martha was distracted with much serving, and she approached Him and said, "Lord, do You not care that my sister has left me to serve alone? Therefore tell her to help me" And Jesus answered and said to her, <u>"Martha, Martha, you are worried and troubled about many things. But one thing is needed,</u> and Mary has chosen that good part, which will not be taken away from her" Luke 10:38-42 (NKJV).

Mortal men are driven by their natural instinct for survival; what they shall eat and drink, what they shall wear, and many of such things that trouble their heart. But immortal men are driven by the quest of their soul to experience eternal realities contained in their spirit's nature in the immortal Christ.

What we see that drives us is not what mortal men see that drives them. What they see is temporary but what we see is eternal.

If an immortal man is driven by what drives mortal men, he is bound by what he sees physically. Such a carnal way of thinking limits him from accessing the wealth of the revelation knowledge of his spirit's nature. This anomaly is the reason for the strife and contention among us. While the revelation knowledge of our spirit's nature produces in us a love walk.

An immortal man who sees with his soul the glory of his spirit's nature in Christ will have his affections for earthly things altered. His affections would henceforth set on superior things above.

> *"Set your affection on things above, not on things on the earth"*
> *Colossians 3:2.*

This should be done intentionally through meditating and contemplating on the living word of God, which is your spirit's nature in Christ until your soul assumes a posture where its affections are only set on things above. What else do you consider a worthy adventure other than having your soul explore the revelation knowledge of the spirit's nature in Christ? This is the ONE NEEDFUL THING.

MIRROR 2.4
The Redemptive Truth Of The Gospel

Know that our spirit's nature in the immortal Christ is the absolute truth, our spirit is LIFE. Our spirit's personality is the word of truth because we are begotten of Him.

The redemptive truth of the gospel is what we became at the new birth experience. The gospel is the revelation of life and immortality, which is the personality of our spirit's nature in the immortal Christ.

The real nature (personality) of our soul and body is the spirit, the alignment of our body with its true nature is the putting on of immortality, likewise our soul. Its renewal is conformity to the revelation knowledge of its immortal nature which is the spirit.

Actually, the exchange of our mortal body for a glorious body is the clothing of our spirit's nature in the immortal Christ. This is how Christ changes our vile body to be fashioned like His glorious body; by dematerializing mortality with the glory of Himself, which is our spirit's nature in Him.

As far as God is concerned, He has completed the work of redemption in Christ, which He consummated into our spirit's nature. In other words, the salvation of our soul and body has been procured in the spirit's nature, which is life immortal in Christ. This is why the redemption of the soul and body is from within our spirit's nature in the immortal Christ.

The revelation knowledge of the spirit's nature beckons on us to set before our heart the glory of our being in its fundamental reality in Christ. This is how we facilitate the work of transforming the soul and exchange of the body.

Mortal reality is a falsehood. It is the complex operative nature of Satan (sin is Satan's life) which had plagued mankind for ages.

MIRROR TWO

This nature of death was the reality of man's spirit after the fall, and consequently, the soul and body were also baptized into this reality of the fallen nature which is death.

Now God was in Christ to TAKE AWAY THIS NATURE; this explains the whole mission behind the birth, death, burial, and resurrection of the Lord Jesus Christ.

> *"For what the law could not do, in that, it was weak through the flesh, God sending his own Son in the likeness of sinful flesh, and for sin, condemned sin in the flesh"* Romans 8:3.

Now in Christ Jesus, our spirit's nature is Life. It is from this civilization of the spirit's nature that the soul will be transformed, and the mortal body exchanged as we continuously behold the knowledge of the glory of the immortal Christ, which is our spirit's nature in Him.

Dear believer, YOU ARE LOVED ETERNALLY.

MIRROR 2.5
THE FULLNESS OF HIMSELF

Dear believer, to be COMPLETE IN HIM is to have His fullness consummated in your spirit.

"For in him dwelleth all the fulness of the Godhead bodily.

> *And ye are complete in him, which is the head of all principality and power"* Colossians 2:9-10.

His fullness encompasses all His realities both within creation and in His uncreated estate. This is the weightiness of the glory of God's immortal life, which is our spiritual nature in the immortal Christ.

Christ is the first begotten from the dead. He was the first new creation of man to be born. He was the first to be made the righteousness of God as a man. We are a new creation (the very righteousness of God) because we are in Him.

We are in Him what He became at the resurrection. This is the reality (the spirit's nature) the soul must be baptized with to experience all the realities of the God-life within and in His uncreated estate.

In that sense, we are still being filled with all the fullness of God, which is embodied in the immortal Christ, but this filling is an experiential immersion of the soul and body into the spirit's nature, which is the FULLNESS OF HIMSELF.

> *"That Christ may dwell in your hearts by faith; that ye, being rooted and grounded in love, May be able to comprehend with all saints what is the breadth, and length, and depth, and height; And to know the love of Christ, which passeth knowledge, that ye might be filled with all the fulness of God"* Ephesians 3:17-19.

Christ dwelling in your heart is the immersion of your soul into your spirit's nature.

We are complete in Him, but our souls are gradually coming into the experience of our completeness in the immortal Christ. Our journey is to arrive at the fullness of ourselves in Him

Identity school of redemption is not basic or one among many truths, IT IS THE TRUTH. It captures this entire journey of the soul to arrive at the complete revelation knowledge of the spirit's nature in the immortal Christ. This is life practice and interactions with one's essence of completeness in the loving Christ by whom we have obtained the inheritance of life and immortality.

YOU ARE THE BLESSED.

MIRROR 2.6
Understanding God Changes Who You Are

Your understanding of God changes by the revelation of your spirit's nature in the immortal Christ. As a result, you would begin to realize that you have a fun loving Daddy. During your times of meditation, He takes you on a walk around the estate of Himself within your spirit's nature.

I love Jesus

Fasting is not a hunger strike, it is an in-depth contemplation in the revelation knowledge of your spirit's nature, where your body is disengaged from material sustenance. The wholeness of your being feeds from one immortal source. In fasting, we actually eat, but we don't feed on mortal substance.

When your body puts on immortality it becomes translucent (probably the best English word to use). The Glory of the spirit's nature becomes the outward shell that houses your body. This is what it means for mortality to be swallowed up of life.

Mortality is the nakedness (a disjoint) of the body from within its true glory nature that houses it. A glorified body is as glorious as a translucent immortal body of man, such that when you see the man, you cannot differentiate between his body and his spirit because both are fused into one indivisible substance.

I said all that, to mean that the concept of man as a tripartite being came about as a result of the fall. Man is not tripartite (three in one) in nature, man is not a spirit that has a soul and lives in a body. Man is a spirit being with a spiritual soul and body fused up into himself as a spirit. The soul and body are spiritual components or interactive tools within the nature of his being as a spirit. Permit me to say that man is singular in nature. He is one whole spirit that has an operative soul and body within him. This will help us to better appreciate our true fundamental essence in the immortal Christ.

MIRROR TWO

MIRROR 2.7
Moment Of Contemplation

There is no ecstatic moment other than the moment of contemplation where your soul feasts on the glory of your spirit's nature in the immortal Christ.

Dear believer, no one truly sees himself in the light of what Jesus became at the resurrection and remains the same. Through the practice of contemplation, the Holy Ghost enlightens our soul with the revealed knowledge of the personality of our spirit in the immortal Christ.

Christianity is the fellowship of gods in the immortal Christ. This is true Christianity driven by the understanding of your spirit's nature. This is the gospel, which is life and immortality that our spirit became at new birth. To preach and teach something else is to mortgage God's redeemed people to satan for a perpetual life of servitude.

When the Church gathers it is for the communion of gods not for ceremonial junks activities.

One of the impacts of what we are being exposed to regarding the revelation of the knowledge of our spirit's nature is that it will cause a revolution within the landscape of the operations in ministries. This revolution is the torrent that will blow off the old system or model of ministries that have made slaves out of the treasured Body of Christ in the presence of our Father.

IDENTITY SERIES - CODE 1

> "Jesus answered them, "Is it not written in your Law, 'I have said you are "gods" If he called them 'gods,' to whom the word of God came—and Scripture cannot be set aside" **John 10:34-35** (NIV).

We step out in love as we litter every nook and cranny with the gospel of life and immortality, which has become our spirit's nature in the immortal Christ.

This has been prophesied by spirit men from all time past, and we see the fulfillment before our very eyes.

These are the days of "gods."

Humbly join the revolution as we cover the earth.

MIRROR 2.8
Our Spirit's Nature Is Christ

Our spirit's nature is Christ the hope of glory. It is the Daystar that arises in our hearts from within our divine essence. Hope is the steadfast assurance of the soul. Without it, the soul will be an object of misery with a vague and frustrating perspective of the ultimate reality of life in its transcendental essence. This forms the cradle by which the ultimate desire for something much more superior and divine is ignited.

MIRROR TWO

The breakthrough begins when we realize that, what the soul languishes and hungers for, is fundamentally our transcendent spirit's nature in the immortal Christ. The hope of glory is the assurance of the soul that it will ultimately experience the glory and completeness of his divine spirit's nature in the immortal Christ.

Our spirit's nature is the glory that God brought forth in the immortal Christ. He does not hope to enter another glory because the fullness of His glory is the present state of the spirit's nature. At present, our spirit's nature is life and immortality.

Some people think that having the hope of glory points to that day when they will come into the bright light of heaven and put on immortality to die no more, rejoicing and singing with angelic choirs forever, worshipping the King of glory. But that's not true, satan lied to us.

This hope in us is a calling of sons to function at the full capacity of the life of God, which is our spirit's nature in the immortal Christ. So the consummation of this hope is not when you die and get to heaven. Death is not the route into glory. Let this sink into you.

Christ as the hope of glory is not a time-bound futuristic experience. The full expression of the glory of the life of God in our spirit's nature is possible to experience now.

The revelation knowledge of your spirit's nature will not make you settle for less. It prepares your heart to receive the fullness of God that is embodied in your spirit's nature.

IDENTITY SERIES - CODE 1

Dear believer, even your soul, and body can experience the full expression of life and immortality in Christ, NOW.

Do you believe this?

MIRROR 2.9
WHAT WE ARE IDENTIFIED WITH?

Our thoughts, actions, and life respond to whatever we are identified with.

Suppose you were in a place where your name was called by someone, you definitely you will respond because you have taken an identity by that name.

The thought of you comes alive in your heart whenever your name is called, even if it coincidentally happens that someone else was being called. This is the fundamental reality underneath the revelation knowledge of your spirit's nature. The way we respond to life situations is based upon the knowledge and image we have of ourselves in the immortal Christ.

When Jesus my Lord said peace be still, and there was a great calm in the storm that confronted them, He wasn't binding and loosing every village witchcraft spirit. He authoritatively superimposed the reality of His inner peace on the storm outside. The revelation knowledge of your spirit's nature guarantees you victory over the storms of life. Greater is your spirit's nature than all the forces of wickedness in the world.

"You, dear children, are from God and have overcome them because the one who is in you is greater than the one who is in the world" 1 John 4:4 (NIV).

When we are offended, we don't respond offensively, we superimpose the reality of our spiritual nature, which is love. We are not like those who show people their "real colour," which by implication they mean retaliation. Our real colour is the spirit's nature. This is to say that identity knowledge is at the root of how we live and respond to life generally.

Dear believer, your personality is your spirit's nature. This is who you are. Dwell on this and allow the beautiful fragrance of your inner essence rises like sweet incense.

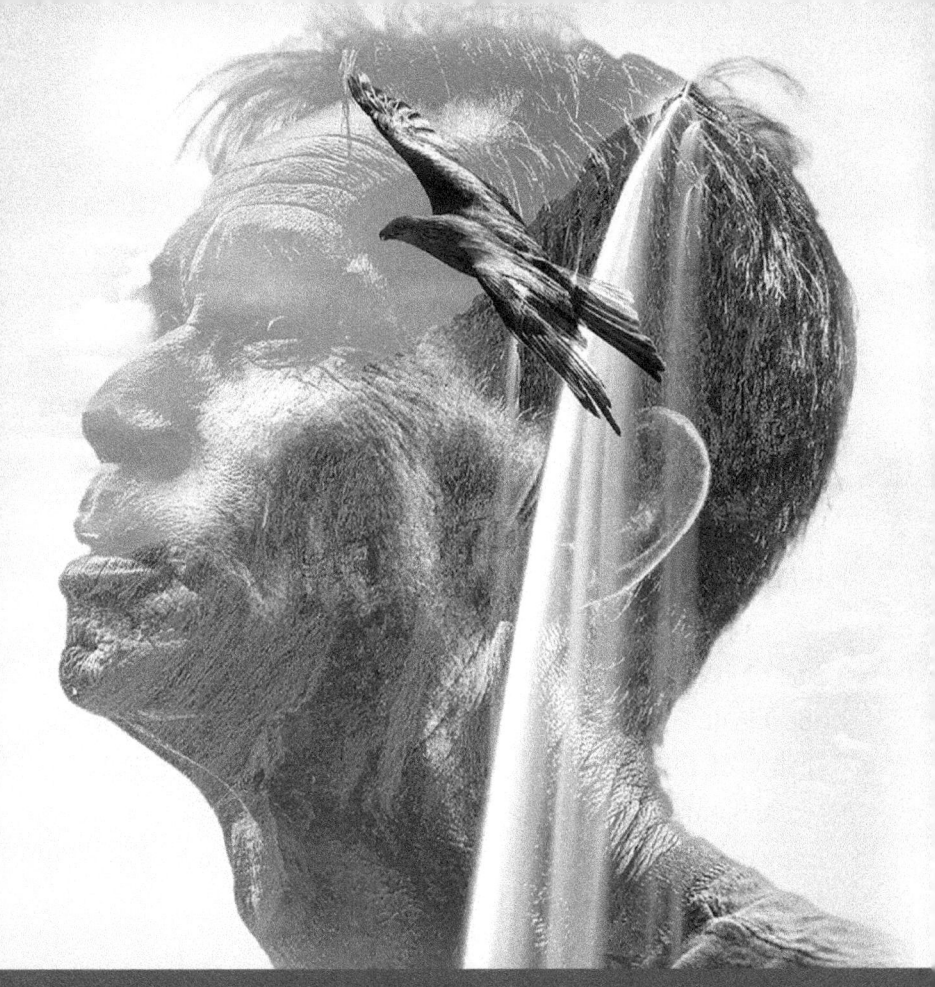

MIRROR THREE
TEACHING SERIES

IDENTITY SCHOOL OF REDEMPTION

IDENTITY SERIES - CODE 1

MIRROR 3.0

God Has Finished His Work

During contemplation, we experience the transcendent nature of our immortal being. This is a communion with the Lord that immerses our soul into the ecstatic river of life that flows from within our spirit's nature in the immortal Christ.

Dear believer, understand that God has finished His work and the result is revealed in our spirit's nature in Christ. But the reality of this God-life (our spirit's nature) is currently being worked out experientially from within us through the revelation knowledge of the Holy Ghost. We are yet to understand the immensity of who we are in Him.

Reason with me.

Do you know that no celestial being can refer to himself as righteousness? Their understanding of righteousness is not the ability to stand before God without any sense of guilt or fear because they don't have any sense of guilt before God. Rather, they see righteousness as the self-embodiment of God by which His life and nature is expressed and experienced.

It is by His righteousness and the word of His power that God upholds all creation in place. Righteousness is God as a mystery

MIRROR THREE

to celestial beings. To them, it is the uncreatedness of God. By His righteousness, God sustains all, yet He is sustained by none.

As the Father is righteousness in Himself, so has He given mankind to be righteousness in Christ immortal.

> *"For He made Him who knew no sin to be sin for us, that we might become the righteousness of God in Him." 2 Corinthians 5:21 (NKJV).*

I am the Living Word of God in Christ by which all creation is sustained. I am life and immortal in the Lord Jesus Christ. I am a wonder man in the immortal Christ. I am not only righteous but much more, I am the righteousness of God in Christ Jesus.

Dear believer, understand me when I said Christianity is the fellowship of "gods" (righteousness).

CAN YOU SEE WHAT I AM SAYING?

MIRROR 3.1
The Beginning Of True Christianity

Beyond just seeing we should perceive. Beyond just hearing, we should understand. Without living out the truth in our daily walk with the Lord, ecstasy with Him remains a mere desire that we wish and sing about, instead of a living experience to enjoy. Having such blissful experience of ecstasy is the yearning of our soul in Christ immortal.

How can we enjoy the Lord without a heightened level of spiritual perception? Contemplation cultivates in us a sense of awareness beyond the level of physicality. It is only in this plane of reality that we can experience the ecstasy of oneness with the Lord.

Dear believer, the blissful ecstasy of oneness with the Lord can't be experienced as long as we remain under the limited boundaries of physicality. We must transcend beyond the consciousness of the physical if we are to experience the joy of the ecstasy of our oneness with Him.

The revelation of the knowledge of our spirit's nature in Christ produces in us this high level of perception through contemplation. Also, our thoughts, desires, and manifestations become cosmic in nature essentially because a level of cosmic consciousness is awakened, so that we don't think in terms of local impact but in terms of universal relevance.

We often say creation awaits our manifestation but what we are not conscious of, is that underneath this manifestation lies INTENTIONAL progressive learnings and recalibration to function outside the matrix system of physicality.

As long as we are still tied down by religious forms of godliness without power, and sense based ways of doing things, creation will continue to hope till we realize the urgency to manifest our spirit's nature in Christ immortal.

MIRROR THREE

When life is all about you, your family, maybe your locality, you don't yet know who you are. The revelation knowledge of your spirit's nature in the immortal Christ births a sense of cosmic consciousness and relevance. In other words, cosmic consciousness and relevance are the side effects of the revelation knowledge of your spirit's nature in the immortal Christ. Contemplation helps you to experience this reality. This is the beginning of true Christianity.

Dear believers, know that you are not a mere human being and should not be limited by the boundaries of the physicality of this material life. You are created to experience higher dimensions and the realities of our existence in Christ immortal.

This is Church life.

MIRROR 3.2
Divine Path Of Ecstasy

When you experience oneness with the Lord, time and space snowball into nothingness. At that point, you are in a plane of reality beyond the physical. This is the ultimate end of contemplation as a pathway.

In as much as I don't condemn 3, 4, 5 or even 10 hours of prayers that most Pentecostal brethren pride themselves with, we must understand that even at our best, we only pray at a very limited plane of reality (time).

Go Beyond That

I stumbled on a video of an Indian mystic recounting his inner life of contemplation. He said he was lost in ecstasy sitting on a chair, and when he was done, he thought he had only spent 25mins. But in reality, the people around told him that he had been sitting on that chair for over three days. He had several of such experiences in his life as a mystic. This is the principles of the kingdom being stolen by the enemy to advance his evil course. What an aberration!

Let me warn you, please don't because of this shy away from this deep level of communion with the Father of all spirits. This is the level of fellowship the Lord desired of us.

Dear believers, we must understand that Christ is both a person and an existential reality, embodying all realms and dimensions of God, unlimited by time and space.

This reality of existence is where we are right now seated together with Him in the heavenly place, far above the reach of the forces of darkness. This is our present position in Christ. But our consciousness needs to align with that reality. Our soul experiencing where we are seated in Christ now is what ascension means to the believer.

MIRROR THREE

It's high time we understand that prayer is not a time for what we think prayer is, but communion in ascension. This is the divine path to ecstasy.

MIRROR 3.3
Believers Have Passed From Death To Life

At the point of new birth experience, we came out of the matrix system of death into an existential reality called life in the immortal Christ.

Dear believer, understand that you have passed from death to life. You are in the kingdom of light now. Your spirit's nature is the uncreated life of God, which is the very source of all creation. Within you are places in God.

Your experiences via communion in ascension through contemplation are from within you. Ascension is transcending physicality into heaven within you. With consistent fellowship and the revelation knowledge of these places within you, unplugs your soul from the matrix system of death.

Our present mortal bodies will perpetually suffer limitations and the experiences of death, as long our soul is still plugged into the matrix of death. Knowledge is how the soul is plugged into the matrix of death. Also, by revelation knowledge of our immortal identity in Christ shall we be unplugged. Hence the need for the mind to be consistently renewed. This is an intentional liberation of the soul from the knowledge of death through the revelation knowledge of our spirit's nature.

- You are life
- You are immortal
- You are not a mere human being
- You are a god being, the very substance of divinity
- You are what Jesus became at the resurrection now
- The word humans describe a race of fallen men in Adam

MIRROR 3.4
Life And Immortality

What we need now is the revelation knowledge of our spirit's nature in the immortal Christ. Looking through history, not much has been unveiled and explored both in knowledge and experience, concerning life and immortality, which captures our life's essence in Christ.

What men described in their limited level of light as moves of God were simply progressions of God, in terms of bringing us to the ULTIMATE IN KNOWLEDGE, which is life and immortality. Unfortunately many are still stuck in those "moves and revivals" discarding this revealed message as a false gospel.

Who Is At A Loss?

What we see now is not one of the many moves; it is the ULTIMATE. This is the generation of FULLNESS. Moves are imperfect compared to the ULTIMATE. When that which is perfect has come, that which is imperfect will be done away with. This is why some practices though may not be wrong, but they are no longer relevant in terms of the new functional upgrade.

That which is perfect is life and immortality, and it has come to stay forever. It is this knowledge that shall cover the earth. This is the truth, and I humbly submit to it.

MIRROR 3.5
The Revealed Knowledge Of Our Spirit's Nature

When Jesus walked on this earth as the son of man, it came to a point in His life when He realized that He is the full expression of the Father. At that point, He could tell people that *"He who has seen Me has seen the Father."* Beyond the surface of His words at that time was the revealed knowledge of the essence of His eternal identity.

Certain statements He uttered was based on the revelation knowledge of His preexistence as God.

Some people think that Jesus was born with the foreknowledge of His Deity automatically. NO! He had no memory of His life essence as God when He was born as a man. This explains why He had to grow in wisdom, in stature, and in favor with God and man, quickened by the Seven Spirits of God operating in His life. Please, this is a very important fact you should know.

> *"Jesus grew in wisdom and maturity. He gained favor from God and people" Luke 2:52 (GW).*

He went through a learning process like we do to download into His soul the revelation knowledge of His personality and preexistence as God.

This revealed knowledge informed His words and actions. He could now say that His words are not mere letters but spirit and life. When He talks, sense-based knowledge men would say He is proudly equating Himself with God.

> *"The Spirit is the one who gives life. The flesh doesn't help at all. The words that I have spoken to you are spirit and are life." John 6:63 (CSB).*

But He was simply a living soul (then He wasn't a life-giving spirit until after His resurrection) who has simply come into the precise knowledge of His life essence as God before eternity was conceived.

MIRROR THREE

It was based on this revealed knowledge that he said, "Father glorify me with the glory which has shared with you before the foundation of the world the world." The "world" here, means all created spheres of existence.

Dear believer, to experience the full stature of our spirit's nature in the immortal Christ is a learning process and a gradual baptism of the soul into the revealed knowledge of our immortal identity. Whoever teaches you otherwise other than this knowledge of our immortal identity is not doing you good. This learning should be ongoing with you both outside and within the close door.

We cover the earth.

MIRROR 3.6
Do You Know Who You Are?

One early morning about 5:00 am, I went outside for morning exercise. While jogging along the road I heard a voice calling for help, so I stopped to trace where the call was coming from. When I eventually got there, it was an aged woman calling for help. I noticed that there were five or six people with her. I asked what was happening to her; they said she always shout calling for help every morning. She has been doing this repeatedly for a few years back.

I then asked the woman what was happening to her. Unfortunately, she couldn't articulate her situation in words but attempted to describe something like a fierce torment and fear that grips her at the early hours of the morning.

I could tangibly feel the oppression around the atmosphere. Immediately an advanced woman of God probably in her 60s came and interrupted me. She said to me nothing is wrong with her, that God wants to use her, but she is refusing to yield to God; that's why she is being tormented by God.

With all due respect, I interrupted her and said no this is not God but an attack of the devil. Then I told her and all around to see what will happen to the woman.

Then I instructed her to stand up from where she was sitting, and she did. Immediately I stretched forth my hands to rebuke the devil, she fell to the ground recoiling herself as though she wants to turn into something else. She did that for about 5mins. To cut the story short, she was delivered at that moment.

After that, we all had a morning devotion together with the woman of God. I taught them the truth of redemption, revealing the nature of the Father. This attack continued unchallenged for such a period just because of ignorance.

Afterward, they asked for my denomination. I told them it is not essential at the moment. The most important thing has been done, so I left to continue my morning exercise.

MIRROR THREE

A large number of believers don't understand the concept of the Fatherhood of God, so they are ignorant when it comes to probing the true state of things and circumstances. This why we go through unnecessary sufferings and sometimes call them "God's dealings." Our ignorance will always make the devil take advantage of us (our ignorance exalt him) and exalts himself as superior. Surely, he is not at all.

The revelation knowledge of our spirit's nature in the immortal Christ births an accurate perspective of the Fatherhood of God. In that reality, you see the devil, destroyed, defeated, disarmed, and dethroned below your feet.

We are not trying to win a battle over satan, he is eternally and irrevocably defeated. (Jesus Christ won the battle already on our behalf). So we walk in victory and dominion to enforce satan's eternal defeat. While many believers are still on a fight with the devil others are simply treading on him. The difference is knowledge.

> *"Behold, I give unto you power to tread on serpents and scorpions, and over all the power of the enemy: and nothing shall by any means hurt you"* **Luke 10:19 (NKJV).**

Do You Know Who You Are?

MIRROR 3.7
The True Nature Of The Supernatural

We miss the true nature of the supernatural life with its blissful impact whenever the gospel is substituted for morality.

The Church is the ground and the pillar of ETERNAL TRUTH; the very center where The manifold wisdom of His uncreated life (our spirit's nature) is revealed and taught to all creation, not the ground of "dos and don'ts."

Today we teach all kinds of morality and call it the gospel. It is a pity. The revealed message of the gospel is clear which is LIFE AND IMMORTALITY.

When believers are taught to live from within their spirit's nature issues of morality will be taken care of. We would live best among ourselves and society at large.

Reason with me.

Today we teach to honour one and another simply because those who dishonour people have no sense of their IMMORTAL IDENTITY.

We don't make side effects the main focus of the message. However, we teach and emphasize this because people have

MIRROR THREE

lost the sanity of who they are. Honour becomes natural to you when the revelation knowledge of your spirit's nature in the immortal Christ becomes a practical reality. Just the same way with walking in love becomes natural for the believer. You will not have to fake it or have the wrong motive for honour. Some do it for the mantle, anointing, and connections, perhaps others for the profundity of the person.

We are trying to teach many things to deal with people's character flaws. That will lead us nowhere. All we need to do is to unveil the knowledge of our spirit's nature so that believers can see themselves in the light of who they are in Christ. Doing otherwise creates an impression that we are busy preaching the gospel, but in the real sense we are just stagnant, making no progress.

We are so busy and preoccupied with so many things but no real advancement of walking in the God-life. This is the present state of the Church; having a form of godliness but without the fruit and reality of the gospel. No corresponding evidence.

But the ULTIMATE has begun, the trump of life and immortality is sounding. This has come to stay. The Church is shining forth, rising in the glory of HER LIFE ESSENCE.

We are covering the earth.

IDENTITY SERIES - CODE 1

MIRROR 3.8
A Believer Is Beyond Human

The stronghold in our soul is the various knowledge by which we have identified ourselves as mere human beings. This knowledge other than the revelation knowledge of your IMMORTAL IDENTITY has taken root in our souls. It takes the entrance of the revealed knowledge of our spirit's nature as "god-beings" to break free from such limitations and its attendant consequences.

Come out from the matrix consciousness and reality of human beings and move into the reality and dimension of "gods."

> *"I have called you all "gods" and "sons of the Most High" Psalm 82:6 (TLB).*

Dear believer you are not man as a human being but man as God being. THIS IS WHO YOU ARE.

MIRROR 3.9
Contemplation

Whenever my soul comes into the bliss of divine ecstasy with the Lord, after contemplation, I feel so burdened and sorry for those whose eyes are

MIRROR THREE

obscured from the truth about life. This is what we seek to bring men into.

A man's life IS NOT IN THE ABUNDANCE OF THE THINGS WHICH HE possesses. This could only be uttered from reality completely strange to men driven by their natural instinct for survival. How can we explore the realities of the world to come that we are in now, without an in-depth consciousness of our true identity?

> *"And He said to them, "Take heed and beware of [a]covetousness, for one's life does not consist in the abundance of the things he possesses" Luke 12:15 (NKJV).*

The knowledge of death has governed the way we think for a long time. It has influenced our view of God, our view of the Church, our definition of success and even the way we run activities.

Communion in Ascension (contemplation) exposes you to the utter vanity of the world and alters your desire and sets your affection on superior things above.

> *"If ye then be risen with Christ, seek those things which are above, where Christ sitteth on the right hand of God. Set your affection on things above, not on things on the earth" Colossians 3:1-2.*

You will then know that the knowledge of death is a system in the soul that runs people's lives and turns them like unto animals whose instinct is only for survival.

The real joy and fulfillment in life is a blissful divine ecstasy with the Lord. THIS IS THE TRUTH ABOUT LIFE. As you go deeper into the practice of contemplation, you will see everything as they are in their untainted state. At this level of reality, greed and passion for mundane things die a natural death. But as long as your soul remain cultured by this system of sin and death, you remain enslaved to it.

When your self-worth is based on fame, career or earthly possessions the knowledge of death is giving you a false identity of yourself. UNPLUG YOURSELF BY A REDEFINITION OF WHAT YOU THINK YOU ARE.

Jesus said life is more than food and the body more than clothing, telling us that though these things are essential, they shouldn't be what we live for. We lose the true essence of life when all these become our pursuit and FOCUS in life.

The spirit beacons on you to come and have an experience of life in its highest reality beyond the matrix of death.

Contemplate to see beyond and live beyond because in truth you are beyond human.

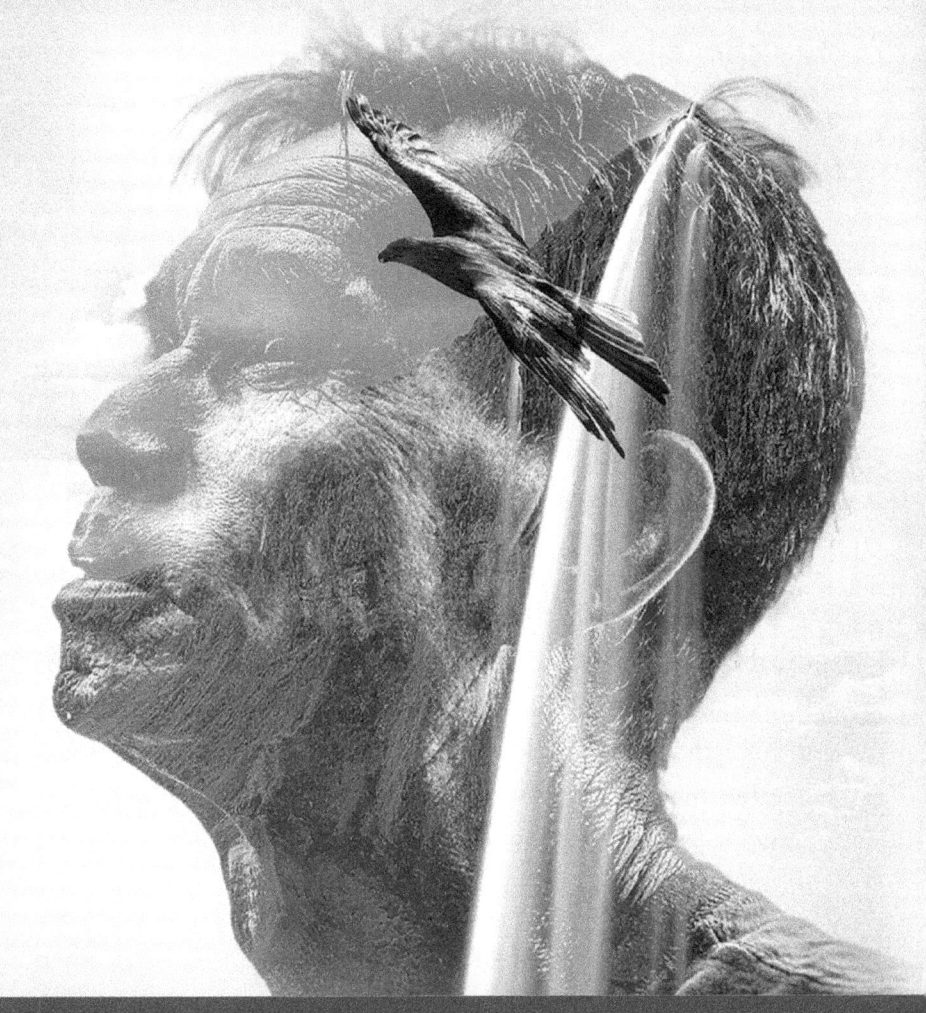

MIRROR FOUR
TEACHING SERIES

MIRROR 4.0
Veil

As I was stepping up to the podium to exhort a group of audience, suddenly, I saw an angel holding a jar in his hand, and he said to me "the capacity of this jar is bigger than an ocean." It was difficult for me to reconcile what he was saying because the jar was tiny.

When he realized that I couldn't comprehend the mystery behind the message, he instructed me to look at the jar from within. As I did, immediately I saw the enormous capacity of that little jar in his hand. As I ponder on that experience for a while, I was granted the privilege to understand the entire message he was conveying to me. That message eventually became the basis for my exhortation to the audience that day.

Brethren, we become small and insignificant in our eyes when we see ourselves from outside of who we are in our spirit's nature. A believer saying that I am an ordinary human being is an aberration and inconsistent with his new nature in Christ. Unfortunately, that believer only sees himself from outside of his life's essence. This is an anomaly and anti-Kingdom way of life that has plagued the 21 century Church.

Look At This More Deeply From Different Bible Translations

"So then, from now on, we have a new perspective that refuses

to evaluate people merely by their outward appearances. For that's how we once viewed the Anointed One, but no longer do we see him with limited human insight" 2 Corinthians 5:16 The Passion Translation (TPT).

"Because of all that God has done, we now have a new perspective. We used to show regard for people based on worldly standards and interests. No longer. We used to think of the Anointed the same way. No longer" 2 Corinthians 5:16 The Voice (VOICE).

"So from now on, we don't think of anyone from a human point of view. If we did think of Christ from a human point of view, we don't anymore" 2 Corinthians 5:16 Names of God Bible (NOG).

"[L So; As a result] From · this time [now] on we do not think of anyone · as the world does [or from a merely human perspective; L according to the flesh]. [L Although] In the past we thought of Christ · as the world thinks [or as nothing more than a man; L according to the flesh], but we no longer think of him in that way" 2 Corinthians 5:16 Expanded Bible (EXB).

"From this moment on, therefore, we don't regard anybody from a merely human point of view. Even if we once regarded the Messiah that way, we don't do so any longer" 2 Corinthians 5:16 New Testament for Everyone (NTE).

Any knowledge other than the revelation knowledge of our spirit's nature gives us a false identity of ourselves. We have to see ourselves with unveiled faces. Religious veil is a kind of knowledge that obscures the truth of your immortal identity. Remember, we have this treasure in an earthen vessel.

Beloved, from today, start defining yourself based on the hidden treasure encapsulated in your earthen vessel not based on the present state of the vessel.

BE TREASURE MINDED.

MIRROR 4.1
God Is With You And In You

You and God coexist and coinhere each other as one indivisible spirit substance. Dear believer, understand that God is with you and in you as one spirit. Know this in your heart. Your spirit's nature now is uncreated. You are eternal life now. You don't grow in your spirit's nature. You only grow in His revelation knowledge, which captures the entire work of soul transformation.

As sons of God ye are gods. Christianity is the fellowship of gods; the father and His family. This is the real "occultism." The occult world is a child's play. We are covering the earth with life and immortality. Nations will come to the brightness of our rising. Dark occult powers of the world will surrender because superior "occultism" has come. DO YOU KNOW WHO YOU?

MIRROR FOUR

MIRROR 4.2
The New Testament

The New Testament is not a set of books chronologically arranged in the Bible after the book of Malachi. "It is the operation of life in the order of the LIFE GIVING SPIRIT initiated by the blood of the slain Lamb at redemption."

It is a living reality in us. This is why the written letter serves as a window. The living word is the reality of your spirit's nature. You are what the Scripture says because the word is your life. You are the word of God in the immortal Christ. The word of truth begot you. You have the DNA of the word. You are incorruptible. You live and abide forever. Dear believer, you are something to shout about!

MIRROR 4.3
The First Adam

The creation of Adam was the first step God took in making man into His image. Unfortunately, that project didn't come to fruition with him. The first Adam before he fell couldn't have been the righteousness of God and die.

"The first man Adam became a living being." The last Adam became a life-giving spirit. 1 Cor. 15:45.

May I now tell you that the first man Adam before he fell was not the image of God. He was just a figure of him (Christ as a life-giving spirit) that was to come.

> **"Nevertheless death reigned from Adam to Moses, even over them that had not sinned after the similitude of Adam's transgression, who is the figure of him that was to come" Romans 5:14.**

The new creation man is the image of the invisible God. He is righteousness. The God-life is incapable of death. It doesn't die. Celestial beings can die in the sense that they can experience separation from the life of God; they are not righteousness.

Righteousness is the God-life. We are God's righteousness. We are life immortal.

May I tell you that any celestial being that rebels against the new creation man experience death. Anything not connected to your spirit's nature is death. You are not only alive; you are life. Your spirit is life, and all creation is alive in you as life.

Can you see what I am saying?

MIRROR FOUR

MIRROR 4.4
We Know The Truth By Communion

You can't know the truth, except by revelation. It takes deep communion and fellowship to encounter the TRUTH. Our Bible study time should be a time of communion not an intellectual dissection of the letters. To rightly divide the word is to see the word as it is; in its untainted state free of intellectualism. You can intellectually dissect the letters, but it takes a heart of communion to unveil the living person of truth. Academic knowledge of the written word without a heart of communion, blurs your understanding of the revealed truth.

The Pharisees know the letter, but they couldn't recognize the person of truth the letter wrote about. So also do the doctors of the law but couldn't see beyond the letter. That is tragic! Such is the state of many today in the Church. Whatever that is beyond their intellectual comprehension they easily disregard.

My Question Has Always Been; Who Is At A Loss?

If you think that only what your intellect can relate with is the truth, wake up and think outside the matrix. You can't deductively arrive at the truth. It is not philosophical. Or better still, when intellect becomes the upfront in our act of philosophical deduction, then philosophy becomes an endless journey of confusion.

The human intellect can't reveal the truth. Only faith can reveal the truth. Faith is never the opposite of ignorance. It is another kind of knowledge; it is the revelation knowledge of the truth, which is born out of the womb of communion. What we call the unity of the faith is a complete revelation knowledge of the truth that we all must come into; that's why it is called unity.

Faith takes you into all the unsearchable dimensions of God's knowledge when you acknowledged the limits of your intellect. Faith is the highest way of learning. It is an ascension where you see things the way they are not as they appear.

This is what happens in contemplation. It gets to a point where you come out of the matrix of intellectual awareness into an exploration of divine mysteries. By the time you are done, you realise something has been imparted into your soul even though you may not yet be able to articulate it intellectually.

Intellect dissects by seeing things the way they appear not as they are. Beyond the intellect, please commune with the living person. If you do, you will save yourself from confusion, unnecessary arguments and stress, because you now know who you believe.

MIRROR FOUR

MIRROR 4.5
Be Intentional About Sticking To Practice

It is essential to note that the expression of the God-life; (our spirit's nature in the immortal Christ) is based on the clarity of revelation knowledge. For the believer to walk in the experience of the God-life, his mind must be consistently renewed with the revelation truth of who he is as righteousness. Always set the truth of your immortal personality before your soul to behold.

Dear believer, you see, the realities of your spirit's nature (the God-life) will not coincidentally be experienced by your soul and body. You must be dogged and intentional to practice it daily. It is by practice we gain mastery to the point that we can easily transcend realms at will.

As you consistently give yourself over to contemplative communion, you will discover how easily you can experience a shift. This is because contemplation is training your soul on how to transcend and travel along the pathway of revelation knowledge with your body, in an undistracted posture.

People are easily distracted and, in some cases, frustrated during contemplation because of the cares in their mind that make it difficult to be still and focus. But don't give up. Stick to the practice. It only gets easier and enjoyable with consistency and commitment. YOU ARE THE BLESSED.

IDENTITY SERIES - CODE 1

MIRROR 4.6
Exposing Your Soul To Light

As you continuously dwell on and expose yourself soul to the revelation knowledge of your spirit's nature in the immortal Christ, you will realise that you are unplugged from certain habits or addiction. Do you realise that you can never be addicted to something you have never been exposed to? In fact, addiction is a result of consistently engaging yourself repeatedly with a particular action. This then births a domineering knowledge (beyond your will power) in your soul called weakness.

The is why you can be in your room with a fierce desire to satisfy the flesh. This inordinate desire could lead you to watch porn videos or masturbate, without contact with the world outside. There is no external factor luring you but a kind of knowledge that has shaped and condition your soul to act and respond to such cravings in a particular manner. Your body experiences whatever form your soul has taken in knowledge.

People asked me how to break free from addiction having try many methods like not hugging the opposite sex, fasting, keeping away from the Internet and so forth. The truth of the matter is that they have never tried enough to set the truth of their immortal identity and dwell on it for long.

MIRROR FOUR

Dear believer, understand that stronghold in the soul is a kind of knowledge, and you would need another higher kind of knowledge to break it off. That higher kind of knowledge is not a legalistic method, it is the revelation knowledge of your spirit's nature in the immortal Christ.

As you engage in contemplative communion, and your soul to dwells on this exposure, you will not struggle to overcome the unrestrained impulse. I guarantee you, that you will undoubtedly walk above it.

THIS IS TRUTH.

MIRROR 4.7
Respond To People By Loving Them

The best way to respond to people is to love them no matter who they are and irrespective of their character flaws. Expressing love is the fragrance of our life essence. It is not a choice, love is our life and the excellent way of living.

Naturally, people just want to find fault with you. Often, they quote you out of context just to make a case against you. Some we will even read your post and find out something you never said in your post. You will be wondering how he/she read the post. But still, we maintain a level of sanity because we now know our words are not just mere alphabet but spirit and life.

And without offense, we bring forth correction with clarity. It is left to them to yield or not. But we should never get to a point where we begin to make a mockery of ourselves with malicious words. Such a practice is not the way of immortal spirits. Remember, we are not merely human beings, so don't act like one. If we do, we may suffer the consequence. Read the scripture below.

> "I have said, Ye are gods; and all of you are children of the most High. But ye shall die like men, and fall like one of the princes" Psalm 82:6-7.

MIRROR 4.8
A Believer Is Righteous

We must realize that we have been made HIS RIGHTEOUSNESS in the immortal Christ. Righteousness is the uncreated nature of His life essence; it is beyond creation's makeup.

At the new birth experience, we were born by this righteousness. We are not at the same level of life as all creation, WE ARE BEYOND.

Dear believer, understand that what we are in our spirit's nature is God's life essence. This is our inheritance through the new birth in Christ. This is why we are the blessed to bless all creation.

MIRROR FOUR

The lesser is blessed of the greater. WE ARE THE GREATER.

The Melchizedek order is an operation of life that pours the fragrance of uncreatedness as a blessing to all creation.

- We are of this order of life.
- We are life-giving spirits.
- We were made to bless all celestial beings and impact all living realities within eternity.

Beyond the cross is the mystic union with DIVINITY. We preach the cross to the world (the old creation) and continue to explore the mysteries of our DIVINE UNION in the new creation. So the message of the cross is not the gospel for the Church but for the world.

It is unfortunate that we have made the Church look like the world. This is one of the reasons we have not so much explore the realities of the God-life.

Let me be precise. For example, you are to tell the world that God is not mad at them, but instead reconciling the world to Himself through Christ.

Unfortunately, at present, this life-giving message is not yet a reality to the Church. We are quick to point the world to the consequences of sin and eternal damnation than to the solution of sin and eternal life in Christ, because we are stuck in the ignorance of the immortal identity of our spirit's nature in Christ.

> *"In other words, God was using Christ to restore his relationship with humanity. He didn't hold people's faults against them, and he has given us this message of restored relationships to tell others. Therefore, we are Christ's representatives, and through us, God is calling you. We beg you on behalf of Christ to become reunited with God" Corinthians 5:17-20 (GW).*

We are yet to comprehend the magnitude of the love of God shared abroad in our heart. Come up higher!

> *"We're not ashamed to have this confidence, because God's love has been poured into our hearts by the Holy Spirit, who has been given to us" Romans 5:5 (GW).*

Often when people say we stick with the gospel but kick against the message of life and immortality, it reveals that what they call the gospel is often what they think is the gospel as opposed to what the gospel truly is. IT IS AN OPINIONATED Gospel.

The world is not the Church, and both should be treated differently. These are two opposing kingdoms.

I was surprised when someone confronted me that I should stick to the message of forgiveness of sins and not life and immortality. I told him that both are all package of the gospel. While the church (or a believer) at her infancy should be grounded and rooted in her knowledge that she has received eternal forgiveness of sins, she must not be stuck there. She must progressively be taught to explore her nature of life and immortality.

MIRROR FOUR

> *"Therefore let us get past the elementary stage in the teachings about the Christ, advancing on to maturity and perfection and spiritual completeness, [doing this] without laying again a foundation of repentance from dead works and of faith toward God"* Hebrews 6:1 (AMP).

In as much as the foundation is critical, but if it becomes the ultimate the full expression of the God-life will remain a dream world. So we must be progressive in revelation knowledge. The spirit beacons on us to advance and step up higher.

> *"After these things I looked, and behold, a door standing open in heaven. And the first voice which I heard was like a trumpet speaking with me, saying, "COME UP HERE, and I will show you things which must take place after this"* Revelation 4:1 (NKJV).

THE EVOLUTION HAS BEGUN!

MIRROR 4.9
The Believers Spirit's Nature Is Righteousness

My spirit's nature is RIGHTEOUSNESS.

- God is love
- God is ageless
- God is immortal
- God is uncreated

- God is all knowing
- I am who God is now
- I am a life-giving spirit
- I am complete and perfect in nature
- I am what Jesus became at the resurrection

Christ is my heaven, and I am already in heaven forever!

I am in the GODHEAD

- God the Father
- God the Holy Ghost
- God the Son
- God the Believer

All together are ONE substance ONE LIFE essence. Our identification is an indivisible union with the uncreated life.

Never mind! Relax! You are free to disagree. You don't have to believe it now, but it is a knowledge you CANNOT escape from. You MUST come to acknowledge it in the journey of arriving at the full knowledge and stature of who you are in HIM. But the sooner, the better.

'In Christ' speaks of UNION where GOD became man and MAN became GOD in LIFE ESSENCE

We are ONE spirit. He is me I am Him.

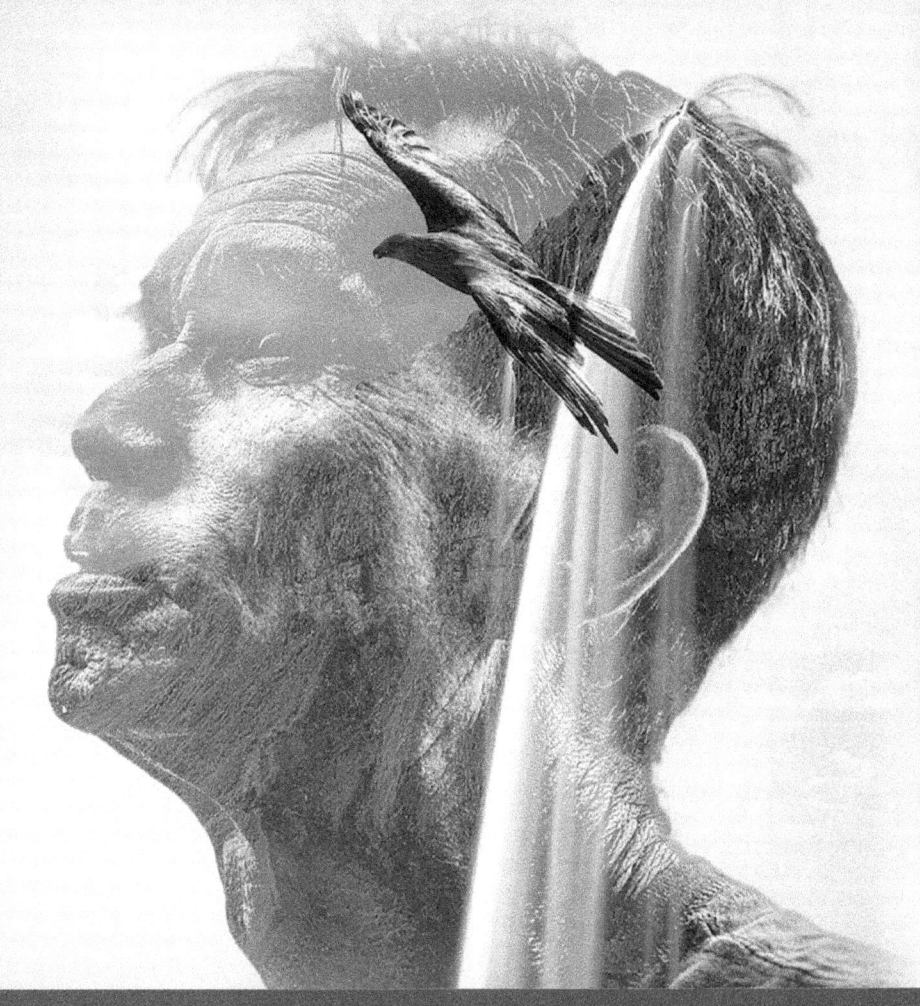

MIRROR FIVE
TEACHING SERIES

IDENTITY SCHOOL OF REDEMPTION | 67

IDENTITY SERIES - CODE 1

MIRROR 5.0
He Is A Life-Giving Spirit

The revelation knowledge of our spirit's nature is all we need now! Do you know that you are what Jesus became at the resurrection? He is life-giving spirit so are you in Him. He is righteousness so are you in Him.

Do you know you are never inferior to Him? You are not "little" Christ you are Christ! Do you know that you are one spirit substance with Him? He is in you, and you are in Him, and both of you are one spirit. You don't have more than one spirit's nature within you! You are not a DUAL NATURE person. Hence;

- Your spirit's nature is Christ
- Your spirit nature's is God
- Your spirit nature's is the Holy Ghost

There is no difference between your spirit and the Holy Spirit; they are INDIVISIBLY ONE SPIRIT SUBSTANCE that CANNOT be separated. Both have been consummated into one spirit's nature at the point of new birth experience! So the Holy Spirit within you is your spirit's nature. You are the ANOINTING! To be anointed with the Holy Spirit is to become ONE spirit with the anointing. He who has anointed us is God.

MIRROR FIVE

No believer is ever more anointed than the other. To think otherwise is utter ignorance. We are all at different levels of expression. In my little journey, I have seen a level of the supernatural in my life, but I always believe that any believer can do the same. This is why I honour men. Most especially those who have gone ahead of me in life and ministry, but I never glory in them.

Do you know why? Because ALL THINGS ARE MINE.

> *"Therefore let no man glory in men. For all things are yours" 1 Corinthians 3:21.*

If we realize this, we will have the right attitude of heart towards men without idolizing them.

You are the blessed.

You are the anointed who has become the anointing because you are one spirit with the anointing.

- One life
- One spirit
- One anointing

This is called union with divinity.

IDENTITY SERIES - CODE 1

MIRROR 5.1
We Behold With An Open Face

An open face by which we behold the glory of the Lord is an unveiled heart through revelation knowledge! The glory of the Lord is the expression of the essence of our life. This expression is the mechanism that facilitates the soul to conform to the image of Christ, which is our spirit's nature and life's essence.

> "But we all, with open face beholding as in a glass the glory of the Lord, are changed into the same image from glory to glory, even as by the Spirit of the Lord" 2 Corinthians 3:18.

This does not mean that the believer is becoming like Christ. We must put this into perspective! The believer is perfect and complete in Christ in his spirit's nature which is the real you. A believer does not experience a change in "nature." He is forever perfected and encased in the Holy Ghost.

Now we are what Jesus became at Resurrection. We are not becoming in the future. But we are progressively being perfected in conduct, which is the expression of our life's essence. Therefore, Christ is being mirrored in our soul and body progressively. This is the ongoing work in our oneness with Him. The reason why the work has been stagnant is now revealed! (truth has escalated).

For too long, our messages have focused on perfecting the believer's imperfect conduct to the detriment of the believer's

MIRROR FIVE

nature in Christ. This misplaced priority has made transformation and change seems impossible. No believer can walk righteously and triumph in life with the sense of guilt and condemnation in his soul. Conduct should not be the message to the believer. It should be the result and effect of the true message, which is life and immortality.

In essence, the message to the believer is life and immortality, which is entirely based on the revelation knowledge of who the believer is in his spirit's nature. We have to consistently behold ourselves in the light of this reality irrespective of our present condition. When we walk in this revelation, change in conduct becomes inevitable.

Our position in Christ is eternal, and our condition is temporal, progressively changing and conforming to His image.

> *"And he raised us up with Christ and gave us a seat with him in the heavens. He did this for those in Christ Jesus so that for all future time he could show the very great riches of his grace by being kind to us in Christ Jesus"* Ephesians 2:6-7 New Century Version (NCV).

> *"For he raised us from the dead along with Christ and seated us with him in the heavenly realms because we are united with Christ Jesus. So God can point to us in all future ages as examples of the incredible wealth of his grace and kindness toward us, as shown in all he has done for us who are united with Christ Jesus"* Ephesians 2:6-7 New Living Translation (NLT).

So for those who assume and criticize that we only preach the message of the perfection of the believer and neglect the ongoing work in the believer's life, are wrong. Just that we are not going about it their own way.

I am a PRODUCT of what I preach (the revelation knowledge of my spirit's nature) it has changed my life for good FOREVER. If you don't go well with my teaching, please IGNORE it and move on with your life as simple as that.

I have been mandated by my LORD to sound the trumpet of the ULTIMATE in Zion, and I am set and focus on doing so.

> *"For do I now persuade men, or God? or do I seek to please men? for if I yet pleased men, I should not be the servant of Christ"* Galatians 1:10.

MIRROR 5.2
A Believer Is The Visible Image Of The Invisible God

The believer is the complex spirit system of divinity that has the fullness of God in him. This spirit's personality called the believer is "man" as a God being. He is Christ. The Bible attests to this reality in 1 John 4:17B;

> *"As he is so are you now."* I am the visible image of the invisible God. If you have seen me, you have seen the Father believeth thou this?

MIRROR 5.3

The Believer's Revelation In The Immortal Christ

The revelation knowledge of who you are in the immortal Christ is all you need to embrace now. I realize that a lot of issues we are trying to fix in the treasured Body of Christ will quickly be taking care of if believers are taught the knowledge of their spirit's identity.

When we come into that fundamental knowledge of our life's essence and true identity, we will not only see ourselves as part of each other's lives but much more, we would see ourselves as ONE life. Therefore, our thoughts, words, and actions will be born out of the revelation knowledge of our UNION as one life.

- No man hates himself
- No man defames himself
- No man dishonors himself
- No man makes a mockery of himself
- No man withholds good from himself

Brethren, we will keep fixing problems in relationship with ourselves, as long as we still have this deep sense of individuality.

We should refrain from some of the languages of the world. Example; something like "see yourself differently from others"

Why should you see yourself that way? I understand that the world loves to preserve and protect their ego and self-esteem. We must not conform to their ways of life.

> *"And do not be conformed to this world, but be transformed by the renewing of your mind, that you may prove what is that good and acceptable and perfect will of God" Romans 12 (NKJV).*

The truth is that immediately you see yourself differently from others your intellect will always want to protect your self-image in all things because it is now all about you.

As a believer why would you even think that you are better off than a fellow believer? Why habour such worldly ambition and way of thinking? With this deep sense of individuality, you hardly see other believer's success as your success or celebrate with them. This world view makes it extremely difficult to appreciate others and identifies with them. This shouldn't be so among us.

With the revelation knowledge of our life's essence we truly come to understand the depth of Jesus' communion with the Father about us:

> *"And the glory which thou gavest me I have given them; that they may be one, even as we are one:" I in them, and thou in me, that they may be made perfect in one; and that the world may know that thou hast sent me, and hast loved them, as thou hast loved me" John 17:22-23.*

Though we may be many, we are one in eternity. This knowledge that WE ARE ONE must be rooted and grounded in our

MIRROR FIVE

consciousness. The world will come to know NOTHING as long as we keep walking on the bases of our individuality. We cannot manifest the God-life in us with this mindset of "this is my ministry that is your ministry," "I mind my business, you mind your business," "I have my life, and you have your life," and so forth. This explains why jealousy and envy easily set in when the other believers are making more progress than we are.

This is one thing I have stayed with overtime most especially in ministry. As long as there is work to be done, I am on the go for it, but if someone gets it done before me, glory to Jesus. The most important thing is that the work is done no matter who gets the credit.

> "I planted, Apollos watered, but God gave the increase. So then neither he who plants is anything, nor he who waters, but God who gives the increase" 1 Corinthians 3:6-7 (NKJV).

Let's not forget that what made us ONE is beyond our earthly preoccupations and ministries.

Unfortunately, we rejoice at each other's fall and mistakes, we explore and expose each other's weakness in other to bring ourselves into the "good picture." These are things we must outgrow among ourselves as we together build a system of synergy that will permeate into systems and every area of existence.

IDENTITY SERIES - CODE 1

MIRROR 5.4

What Happened At New Birth?

At the new birth experience, the nature of the old man was utterly terminated. The cross didn't improve on it, it ended your life in the old creation. After the work of the cross, you were quickened back to life with resurrection power having been made RIGHTEOUSNESS. In your spirit's nature, you never existed before. Your kind is GOD Himself because you were begotten by Him.

> *"Being born again, not of corruptible seed, but of incorruptible, by the word of God, which liveth and abideth for ever."* 1 Peter 1:23 (KJV).

Now Here Is The Aspect I Want To Deal With

The part of your soul that contained all the experiences you had in your old ways of life is called the memory, which is part of the soul's makeup. It is the file where past transactions are stored. Unfortunately, your soul didn't experience an instant change like your spirit. It requires a continuous renewal of the mind to delete the records of the previous transactions of your soul.

Do you know how many people are under torment today because they are imprisoned in their past memories? Understand that those past experiences exist today only in the form of memories. Though they are not real anymore but can influence the realities

MIRROR FIVE

of today. Some believers are currently under torment from their past experiences because they see life through the lens of their memory. Hence, they view themselves based on those nonexistent sufferings of the past. As a result, their past memories influence and determine their present actions, reactions, and responses to life. What a tragedy?

The stronghold of the memory of your past experiences is broken via a redefinition of who you are based on your present spirit's nature through revelation knowledge. Understanding this present reality of your spirit's nature facilitates experiences based on the newness of life. You must not define yourself based on the past which merely exists as a memory in your soul.

As you continuously feed on the truth of who you are now in your spirit's nature, enormous transforming works happens within the region of your soul, such that history remains in its grave where it belongs. If you are suffering from any past experiences in your life, I want you to think about what I just said.

You are NEW.

IDENTITY SERIES - CODE 1

MIRROR 5.5

Contemplative Communion

Contemplative communion helps us to focus more on our innermost being and experience a blissful romance with the Lord! At this point, our consciousness of the material world becomes less important.

Ascension is a dimensional shift in consciousness from the limited boundary of physicality into the boundlessness within our spirit's nature. From within that boundless plain of reality, we see things the way they are not as they appear to be.

If we must transverse and navigate in the realms of God which are constituted within the boundlessness of our spirit's nature, we must learn and acknowledge contemplative communion as the way of ascension.

It is unfortunate today that among many denominational circles, the end result of prayer does not always lead to experiencing ecstatic intercourse with the Lord. Instead, prayer is either about binding and loosing, killing of witches and wizards that hinder their progress in life. To some others, it is all about asking God to protect and do something for them. Yet to others, prayer is to enable them to manifest power and "increase" the anointing. They call it "paying the price for the anointing."

MIRROR FIVE

In this respect, none of the above is a substantial reason for prayer. The essence of prayer is deep and contemplative communion with the Lord that flows from our spirit's nature in Christ immortal.

I don't think many would still pray if there is no devil to fight, no demon to cast out, no fear of insecurity because such has been the object of their prayers, Dear believer, let prayer be a love communion with your Father.

Today many will not fast until they have an invisible "mountain" blocking the advancement of their destiny. But fasting becomes a joyful and most productive exercise when it is towards the exploration of your life's essence in contemplative communion. You just easily get caught up in blissful ecstasy (you become timeless in your consciousness).

How pathetic to know that some believers pray to earn the title "Prayer Warrior." They just enjoy the feeling of praying for hours even though they don't have substantial interactive experience with the Lord. They feel accomplished by telling you how many hours they prayed. To them, effectiveness in prayer is the amount of time spent in prayer. How ridiculous it is to relegate prayer to the length of time spent praying.

Prayer is a time of fellowship and interaction with divine truths. It is how we consciously come into timelessness. If the deep within the core of your being is calling you higher, then you must descend into your depth via ascension.

You cannot continue doing the same thing and expecting a different result. Is time for you to make a drastic change and experience the depth of your life's essence in prayer.

To me, contemplative communion is not one type of prayer; IT IS PRAYER.

MIRROR 5.6

Confession

We are covering the earth with the knowledge of life and immortality. Hallelujah!

- I am life
- I am love
- I am divine
- I am "god"
- I am uncreated
- I am righteousness
- I am one spirit with the Lord
- I am what Jesus became at the resurrection!
- We dare to look into the depth of our life essence
- We dare to speak concerning the reality of our union with divinity

MIRROR FIVE

MIRROR 5.7

Taking The First Step In Supernatural Leading

One day I was on a public bus, and an advanced woman was sitting in front of me. Immediately the Lord asked me to accompany her wherever she stops. That wasn't really a convenient thing for me to do having fixed all my mind on my final destination, but I had no choice than to prepare myself to stop. Unfortunately for me, her final destination was nowhere close to where I was going to. After she dropped, I was still in the bus thinking on what to do next. When the driver drove off, I immediately asked him to stop and disembarked. Quickly I ran to catch up with the woman. As I approached her, she began stirring at me with a weird look.

Getting to her, I introduced myself and suddenly the word family drop on my heart. I told her that the Lord would have me discuss and pray with her. Fortunately, she gave me permission. As we talked, she said that she lost the husband a few months ago, her children are battling with health challenges, and all other family responsibilities were resting on her.

I then prayed with her not minding whether we were in the public place or not. After that, she was exceedingly comforted with the word of counsel from the womb of the spirit.

Sometimes the leadings of the supernatural comes when taking the first step is most inconvenient to us;. However, we must learn to always respond first and think later.

IDENTITY SERIES - CODE 1

I notice that as we delay at responding to promptings the more unreasonable and senseless the particular leading becomes and most times, we end up not acting on such leading. This is why our first response to supernatural leading must be action rather than reasoning.

After I was done, I knew she has been touched unimaginably, and my journey back to my destination was full of joy.

MIRROR 5.8
What Is Simplicity?

The reason why I always make use of certain words in my posts is that certain words CREATE SPACE FOR YOU TO THINK BIGGER.

Don't forget that our English language is still developing and expanding, and it is actually difficult trying to capture eternal realities in words within our limited vocabularies. This is why I differ with those who think simplicity is in WORDS. But I believe simplicity is God's nature, not articulation.

Like the English word "love" many people only know love in its language definition but not many know WHO love is in His person. Love is actually beyond human comprehension. What then do you call something that is beyond human comprehension? Love is a mystery. Hence its simplicity is spirit, not letters.

MIRROR FIVE

Let say the word "uncreated life" it simply means eternal life. Do you know that the word eternal does not perfectly capture the life of God? It was adopted to capture the exact life of God because that was the best word that could be used to describe it.

Eternal life in its English meaning means living forever: a life that is living forever! That couldn't have been all about eternal life because EVERYTHING God created is living forever.

Created spirits are eternal beings they are forever living! God does not share the same life with created spirits beings, yet we say His exact life is eternal life. Really, God is not just an "eternal being" saying that puts Him on the same level with created spirits beings! Don't get so sticky with the letters that you cannot see beyond them!

> *"He has made us competent as ministers of a new covenant—not of the letter but of the Spirit; for the letter kills, but the Spirit gives life" 2 Corinthians 3:6 (NIV).*

So when we begin to replace "eternal life" with "uncreated life," this is to allow you to think on the bigger picture. I don't encourage the use of intellect to understand spiritual realities. You must engage your spirit for accurate discernment and comprehension.

> *"For this reason, we also, since the day we heard it, do not cease to pray for you and to ask that you may be filled with the knowledge of His will in all wisdom and spiritual understanding" Colossians 1:9 (NKJV).*

Real understanding is underneath words, so SEE BEYOND just words. We are spirit people.

IDENTITY SERIES - CODE 1

MIRROR 5.9

Stay On The Revelation Knowledge Of The Truth

Stay on the revelation knowledge of your spirit's nature. Don't bother yourself with change. Change and transformation are the obvious consequences of your commitment to the divine order. The order is beholding the finished work of God in your spirit's nature, which should be your only concern and responsibility as a believer.

> *"Jesus answered and said to her, "Martha, Martha, you are worried and troubled about many things. BUT ONE THING IS NEEDED, and Mary has chosen that good part, which will not be taken away from her" Luke 10:41-42 (NKJV).*

> *"One thing I have desired of the Lord, That will I seek: That I may dwell in the house of the Lord all the days of my life, to behold the [b]beauty of the Lord, and to inquire in His temple" Psalm 27:4 (NKJV).*

Understand the one thing that is needful and stick to it.

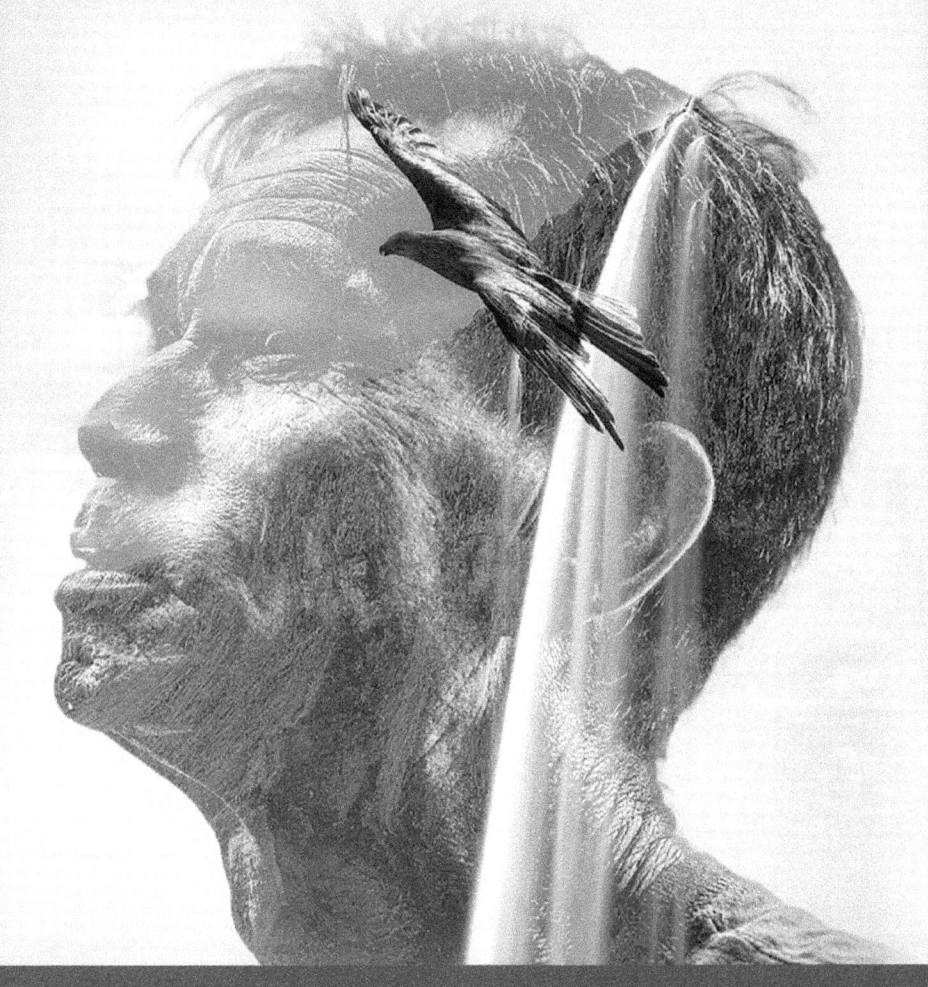

MIRROR SIX
TEACHING SERIES

IDENTITY SERIES - CODE 1

MIRROR 6.0
Embrace Teachings That Reveal Your Spirit's Nature

When I discovered that my responsibility is to set my soul to behold my immortal personality in Christ, I had to let go of distractions. If any teaching fails to reveal who I am in my spirit's personality, I let it go. I don't dwell on it because it would becloud my perception and distort my true identity in Christ.

Most things we struggle with in life would be easily taken care of if we consistently set the revelation knowledge of our spirit's nature as the mirror for our soul. This is the key to an everlasting transformation. This is my message to believers.

MIRROR 6.1
The Anointing Abiding In Him

Your spirit's nature is the anointing abiding in you. He is the Spirit that we received of God that we might know the THINGS that are FREELY given to us of God.

"Now we have received, not the spirit of the world, but the spirit which is of God; that we might know the things that are freely given to us of God" 1 Corinthians 2:12.

MIRROR SIX

Contrary to popular opinion, you are not COMING into fullness. Fullness is your PRESENT state in Christ. You are only coming into its KNOWLEDGE progressively in your soul. This is what it means to be filled with all the fullness of God. It is the epignosis (full complete knowledge) of your spirit's nature being engraved in your soul by the Holy Spirit as you behold yourself in Christ.

Your spirit doesn't grow in understanding. Your spirit possesses a complete knowledge of all things which is the mind of Christ.

> *"For who hath known the mind of the Lord, that he may instruct him? However, we have the mind of Christ" 1 Corinthians 2:16.*

We are NOT going to have but have it ALREADY. Exploring the mind of Christ is exploring the reality of our spirit's nature. You must understand who a believer is in Christ. Your spirit's nature is the unction from the Holy One.

> *"But ye have an unction from the Holy One, and ye know all things" 1 John 2:20.*

Notice it didn't say you shall, will, or can know all things, but it said YOU KNOW ALL THINGS. Your spirit's nature is the anointing that teaches your soul all things as you set your soul to BEHOLD HIM continuously. You may want to say the Holy Ghost is the anointing, not my spirit. I do not disagree with you either. However, you are free to differ with me.

But know that the anointing which you have received of Him ABIDES in you. This means that it has become ONE with you. Your spirit's nature is the anointing within you.

Understand that what you call your spirit is not different from the Holy Spirit. Never mind if you don't agree. Just pretend as if you do. A believer does not have a dual nature or spirit personalities within him. He doesn't have two different spirits (his spirit and Holy Spirit) in him. Both what you call your spirit and the Holy Spirit has been consummated as one spirit substance. It is this one spirit substance that some call the recreated human spirit. They are indivisibly one substance in the spirit.

Do You Truly Know Who You Are?

- I am one with the anointing
- I am one with divinity

I see a generation of the ultimate whose understanding of Christianity is the fellowship of gods! God was glad in Christ to share the glory of His life essence with me, and my mouth is wide open to declare His goodness.

Hallelujah!

We cover the earth.

MIRROR 6.2
Foundation Has To Be Laid

Certain truths about the new creation man were not explored in detail by the Apostles in the gospel, but we can see them scattered all around in the epistles. This was not a mistake because the FOUNDATION had to be laid first. For those who have the eyes to see, they can see the patterns being joined together and the laying down of a precept for another precept, which ultimately becomes the COMPLETE STRUCTURE.

MIRROR 6.3
God Put All Of Himself Into Redemption

Don't forget that God put all of Himself into redemption so that the UNION with DIVINITY would be a possible reality for man.

Our Union with Him is oneness with His life essence.

- We are life
- We are his wisdom
- We are his righteousness

At your new birth experience, God brought forth an uncreated being of Himself. God was so glad to make you one with Himself in Christ. You are one spirit with LORD. This is why you are special.

MIRROR 6.4
Beholding

The mechanism for transformation of the soul is BEHOLDING yourself in the light of what Jesus became at the resurrection. Now that you are in HIM, do you see yourself as Him? Your identity now is the person of the living Christ. Whatever that He is not can never be you.

MIRROR 6.5
The Mirror In Which He Sees Himself

Your spirit's nature should be the mirror by which you see yourself. That is your reality. It should be the basis of your interaction with life in general. You are in life. There is no death in you. For you to think death is an aberration. It is giving the devil the freedom to work the experiences of death in you. Never do that to your precious self. The spirit's reality of the believer is the testimony of God's finished work

MIRROR SIX

in Christ. It is the testimony of the God-life consummated into your spirit's nature.

- You are eternal life
- You have become one with Him
- Eternal life is the person of God

Do you realize that you don't have different spirits within you? What you call "your spirit" is a consummation of the human recreated spirit and the Godhead as one indivisible spirit substance. This is identification.

- One life
- One faith
- One spirit
- One nature
- One throne
- One authority
- One righteousness

Who you are is what Jesus became at the resurrection.

IDENTITY SERIES - CODE 1

MIRROR 6.6

The Sanctifier And The Sanctified Are One Spirit

Both the sanctifier and those who are forever sanctified are one spirit's nature. We are from Him, and we are ONE with Him FOREVER. If you don't agree with me, relax. Salvation is NOT a process; it is a ONE-time experience. Now it is clear that your soul is still being renewed and your body is still mortal. The soul being saved means renewal. This implies that it is a process. However, this does not in any way suggests that your salvation is a process.

The you that was saved instantaneously FOREVER is the spirit. That is your personality (who you are) the real you. It is wrong to say a believer is being saved and he shall be saved. The reason why you are a believer is that you are saved. In other words, you can not be a believer unless you are saved. To say this is to separate him into three persons, which is an error.

The possibility of renewing your soul and exchanging the mortal body is because you (spirit or the person) have been saved. Your soul is being renewed because you have been saved. Your soul is not a separate person that is still being saved; it is just the expressive tool of the saved person that is still being renewed now.

How is the soul being saved or being renewed? By beholding (revelation knowledge in the heart) the true nature of its person (you spirit's personality), even the exchange of the mortal body is from within your spirit's reality. Your spirit's nature is the life that will swallow up death in your body.

You are eternally saved.

MIRROR 6.7
Man Is A Spirit, Possessing A Soul And A Body

Man is a spirit personality who possesses a soul and a body as his spiritual instruments to express himself as a spirit being. He is not tripartite in nature; his soul is not a separate person; neither is his body. It is wrong to say that the spirit is the part of man that is saved, no sir. The spirit is the whole man. Man is a full-fledged spirit being with a soul and body.

However, the wholeness of his being as a spirit is the total conformity of his soul and body to the full reality of himself as a spirit being. This is what Paul meant in 1 Thessalonian 5:23.

Dear believer, you are forever blameless as a person in the presence of your Father, irrespective of the present state of your soul and body. Your soul and body being blameless is their full conformity to the reality of life and immortality, which is your spirit's nature (the real you).

Your spirit's nature is COMPLETE divinity, which requires the soul and body to come to full alignment with himself to completely find expression. They are not separate persons. They are conduits for you as a spirit personality to express yourself. This alignment of the soul and the body is through revelation knowledge of who a believer is. (Immortal Personality)

As an immortal personality;

- You are immortal
- You are forever saved
- You are forever complete
- You are forever sanctified
- You are forever blameless
- You are one with the anointing
- You don't just have life in you; you are life eternal

The unction from the Holy one has become one with you. So you know all things.

MIRROR SIX

MIRROR 6.8
Do You Know Who You Are?

Christ is not sitting on a throne beside the Father's throne neither the believer besides Christ's throne. There is no more than one throne in heaven above all others. Do you get that? We only have one throne above all — this one throne in heaven.

- God the Father is sitting on it
- God the Christ (son) is sitting on it
- God, the Holy Ghost, is sitting on it
- God, the believer, is sitting on it

We are seated together with Christ in heavenly places. Wherever Christ is, there we are. This is called identification. The throne is the family business of the Godhead, which the believer is part of.

- One life
- One spirit
- One Glory
- One righteousness
- One throne (Dominion, government)

Wait! Do you know who you are?

IDENTITY SERIES - CODE 1

MIRROR 6.9

Desire Truth

Some people want to play along with the existing structure. That's not a very good way to live. Stand your ground and blow the trumpet for the new day that has come upon us. No man has ever been relevant who merely want to play along with everybody. Let your loyalty to TRUTH be known to all.

As much as it is possible, love and honour everyone, but never expect the same from others. You stand a chance of losing nothing if they act otherwise.

Until your desire for truth becomes stronger than people's praise, you will never stand the test of time. Selah!

Some praises are disguised attack to keep you perpetually in ignorance. However, the moment you are enlightened and ready to identify with the truth irrespective of men's commendation, challenges will come against you.

Sometimes, you may be ignored and regarded as "nobody." Directly or indirectly, spoken against, because you are less concerned about the praises of men, those attacks no longer affect you. That's why we must continue and never give up. Eventually, others will come to acknowledge that they can't fight the truth forever.

MIRROR SIX

It takes men of courage, consistency, and firmness to break out of the existing structure that has brought us to nowhere. Men of eternal relevance have once in their lifetime been ignored and regarded as nothing. Some were labeled false and mischievous, but they never gave up instead stayed through for the truth.

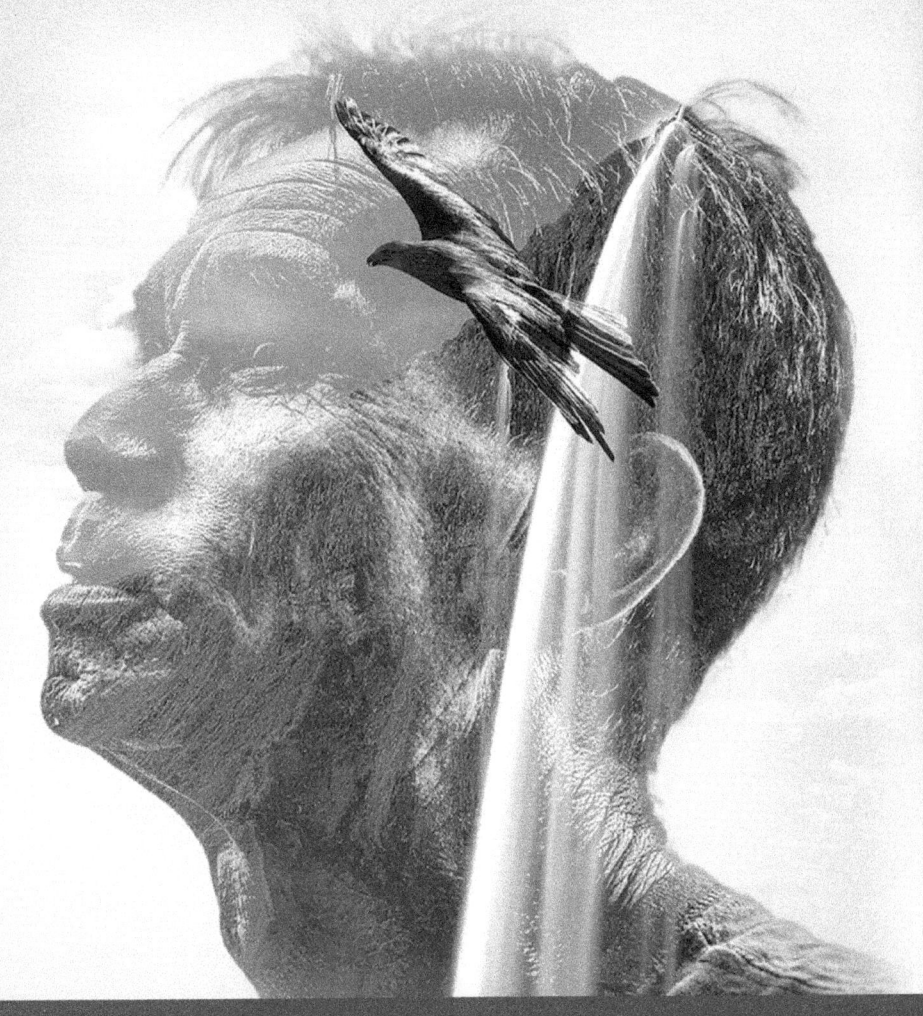

MIRROR SEVEN
TEACHING SERIES

IDENTITY SCHOOL OF REDEMPTION

IDENTITY SERIES - CODE 1

MIRROR 7.0
Christianity Is The Fellowship Of Gods

How do you plug into that ever-flowing river of God? It is by maintaining the consciousness of who you are in your spirit's personality. Then you will realise that you are actually the river of God. Your spirit's nature is the river of life. So where we draw from is from within us not outside of us. You are what Jesus became at the resurrection.

MIRROR 7.1
I And My Father Are One

The Jews understand what it means to say that "I AND MY FATHER ARE ONE" than so many believers.

"I and my My Father are one. Then the Jews took up stones again to stone him. Jesus answered them; Many good works have I shewed you from my Father; for which of those works do ye stone me? The Jews answered him, saying, For a good work we stone thee not; but for blasphemy; and because that thou, being a man, makest thyself, God. Jesus answered them, Is it not written in your law, I said, Ye are gods? If he called them gods, unto whom the word of God came, and the scripture cannot be broken; Say ye of him, whom the Father hath sanctified, and sent into the world, Thou blasphemest; because I said, I am the Son of God?" John 10:30-36.

MIRROR SEVEN

Jesus said if the people to whom the word was given were called gods what about Himself who has been sanctified and sent into the world? Now as the new creation man the word of God is not coming to you from outside you. Your spirit's nature is the very living word of truth begotten of God. You are the very word in the lips of your Father.

> **"Of his own will begat he us with the word of truth, that we should be a kind of firstfruits of his creatures" James 1:18.**

Christianity is the fellowship of GODS. We are one spirit substance with the Father.

MIRROR 7.2
We Are Gods

- I am the river of life
- I and my Father are one
- I am the presence of God
- I am one with the anointing
- I am one spirit with the Lord
- I am the visible image of God
- I am one life with the Godhead

His presence is the expression of my spirit's nature.

If you have seen me, you have seen the Father. My Father and I are one. My words are spirit life. I refuse to condescend to accept a false knowledge and misrepresentation of who I am in Christ, for I am what Jesus became at the resurrection. Observe the words of Jesus in the scriptures.

> *"Yet ye have not known him, but I know him: and if I should say, I know him not, I shall be a liar like unto you: but I know him, and keep his saying. Your father Abraham rejoiced to see my day: and he saw it, and was glad" John 8:55-56.*

We are not speaking falsely about ourselves, in fact, to say anything otherwise of who we are is to disregard the testimony of truth concerning us. We know who we are in Him. As He is now, so are we at present.

Question!

Who Is Jesus Now?

Do you see yourself in that light? If you don't, ask the Holy Spirit to enlighten your understanding so you can comprehend the depth of this identity matter. Jesus said to us that when the Holy Spirit comes, He will guide you into all truth.

> *"However, when He, the Spirit of truth, has come, **HE WILL GUIDE YOU INTO ALL TRUTH;** for He will not speak on His own authority, but whatever He hears He will speak; and He will tell you things to come" John 16:13 (NKJV).*

Apostle Paul had a similar experience at his conversion. The Lord Jesus told him of things He will yet reveal to him.

MIRROR SEVEN

"But rise and stand on your feet; for I have appeared to you for this purpose, to make you a minister and a witness both of the things which you have seen and OF THE THINGS WHICH I WILL YET REVEAL TO YOU" Acts 26:16 (NKJV).

MIRROR 7.3
The Revelation Of Your Immortal Personality

Brethren reason with me.

Can you observe the way Jesus walked the earth as a living soul being?

- Can you see that He was God over darkness?
- Can you see that He was God over nature?
- Can you see that He was God over lack?
- Can you see that He was God over life?
- Can you see how He spoke?

The Bible said He taught as one with authority.

- Can you see how he represented the father?
- Can you see how he handle those around him including the religious forks?

It was said of him "no man ever spoke like this." He was indeed a wonder-man. When you look at Him, you are almost compared to be like the Jesus that walked the street of Jerusalem. Much more we have the resurrected Christ who has been made higher than the heavens. We know Him no more after the flesh but after the order of Him as the life-given spirit.

I want to have a testimony concerning my words. So that when I speak, they would say; "he speaks like God, as one with authority, like Jesus." When the unbeliever say I am proud, I understand him. So did they in Jesus' day because they are blind. However, when the redeemed says I talk as if I am God and therefore draws a conclusion that I am proud, I will lament for them because they have denied the testimony of truth concerning themselves.

WE ARE GODS:

- There are ways gods see
- There are ways gods act
- There are ways gods live
- There are ways gods talk

MIRROR SEVEN

MIRROR 7.4
What Is The Gospel?

Now I don't bother myself with knowing too many things. If it is not the revelation knowledge of my immortal personality, I don't need it. Never see through the lens of the knowledge that speaks less of your spirit's nature in the immortal Christ. It would help if you preciously filtered what comes into your soul faculty. Your goal shouldn't be to acquire much knowledge about many things. You will not win an award or conquer death in your soul and body just by the vast of knowledge you amass in your head.

Besides the knowledge of your spirit's personality within your soul faculty, other forms of knowledge are bringing you into conformity with death. This is why you must be disciplined with what you listen to and what you set eyes to read. It is as critical as that.

Beware, many people are out there hiding under the coverage of "preaching the gospel and talking kingdom," they will tell you everything other than who you are as an immortal personality in Christ. Be wise and contend for what comes to stay in your soul faculty, lest you be confused, discouraged and eventually be wearied in your soul.

IDENTITY SERIES - CODE 1

MIRROR 7.5

Believers Co-Exist And Co-Inhere As One Immortal Spirit

Our gospel is not problems generated gospel, but we do know that it is life and peace to anyone who dares to believe it.

What Is This Gospel?

- It is life and immortality
- It is not man's opinion

It is the revelation of Jesus Christ that captures what a man became in his spirit's nature at the new birth experience. This same gospel is actually the revelation of the believer's identity with the Godhead

- This same gospel is the revelation of the believer's identity as righteousness

- This same gospel is the revelation of the believer's identity as love

- This same gospel is the revelation of the believer's identity as light

- This same gospel is the revelation of the believer's identity as glory.

MIRROR SEVEN

- This same gospel is the revelation of the believer's identity as immortal.

- This same gospel is the revelation of the believer's identity as life eternal.

- This same gospel is the revelation of the believer's identity as life-given spirit.

- This same gospel is the revelation of the believer's identity as the son of God.

- This same gospel is the revelation of the believer's identity as the song of all creation.

- This same gospel is the revelation of the believer's identity as an uncreated spirit personality.

- This same gospel. This same gospel. This same gospel reveals the believer's identity as Christ.

- This same gospel is the revelation of the believer's identity as the living word in the lips of the Father.

- This same gospel is the revelation of the believer's identity as the new creation man who never existed.

MIRROR 7.6

Believers Are What Jesus Became At The Resurrection

Do you know what it means for the Holy Ghost to dwell in you? It doesn't say that you now have two different spirits in you (your spirit and the Holy Spirit). It is that both collapsed into one indivisible spirit substance. They are one spirit now. Your spirit's nature is the Holy Spirit now. You both eternally co-exist and co-inhere each other as one immortal spirit. The Holy Spirit dwelling in you is you as a life-given spirit.

Do you know what it means to quicken your mortal body by the Spirit dwelling in you? It means to swallow up the mortal body by life. Your spirit is life.

> "So then they that are in the flesh cannot please God. And if Christ is in you, the body is dead because of sin; but the spirit is life because of righteousness. But if the Spirit of him that raised up Jesus from the dead dwell in you, he that raised up Christ from the dead shall also quicken your mortal bodies by His Spirit that dwelleth in you" Romans 8:8, 10-11.

The body putting on immortality is employing the Spirit of Christ within you (your spirit personality). The appearing of the Lord to change our mortal body is from within us not from the sky.

> "And so we have the prophetic word confirmed, which you do well to heed as a light that shines in a dark place until the day

MIRROR SEVEN

dawns and the morning star rises in your hearts" 2 Peter 1:19 (NKJV).

Moreover, time is not a yardstick for His appearing. It is clear that the quickening is by the Spirit dwelling in you, so it is a possibility both for now and the future. You don't have to die first before you can experience this transformation from mortality to immortality in relation to the body.

Some believers like Martha are waiting for the day of resurrection while the person of resurrection is right now within them. With the person of resurrection, both past and future time are collapsed into now. That's why all the possibilities in God are ever now. God is not telling anyone to wait for the future.

"For if ye live after the flesh, ye shall die, but if ye through the Spirit do mortify the deeds of the body, ye shall live" Romans 8:13.

Study that in context. The death resulting from living after the flesh is the death of the mortal body, not the spirit (an immortal spirit cannot die any form of death). However, to live from your spirit's personality is what enlivened your body beyond death. The mechanism to exchange your mortal body is your spirit's nature; this is righteousness.

MIRROR 7.7
The Glory Of The Latter House

You are what Jesus became at the resurrection. For you to be functional, the revelation knowledge of your spirit's personality must be first imparted in your soul faculty.

"That the communication of thy faith may become effectual by the acknowledging of every good thing which is in you in Christ Jesus" Philemon 1:6.

Acknowledging every good thing that is in you in Christ Jesus is an enlightened heart posture of honour concerning what had been wrought in your spirit's personality. You don't really know what true honour is when you lack the revelation knowledge of your immortal identity (spirit's personality) in Christ. Our fellowship in the spirit thrives on the revelation knowledge of who we are in the spirit.

As ministers of the mysteries of God, our calling is to expose the heart of the saints to who they in their spirit's personality. Our service in the fivefold ministry in the New Testament is to build the saints by exposing them to the light of who they are in the sense of what Jesus became at the resurrection.

You are not to preach what you feel like preaching. You should not even allow problems to affect the purity of your service as a minister of the oracles of God (many people don't know this).

MIRROR SEVEN

God didn't send anyone to focus on the problems, maybe in the believers' lives and make them the central focus of your message. No sir. I disagree. Changing anybody is not your responsibility. Only doing the necessary thing is your responsibility. Change is an obvious consequence of a commitment to a due process.

As you stick to the task of unveiling the truth of the believers' identity to the heart of the believers, the adjustment and change God so desire will happen. Exposing and teaching the truth of the believer's spirit's personality is life-changing power.

Oh, how my heart longs for those who will be consistent with this task without distraction. It is by the sounding of this trump (this message) that sons will emerge. Selah!

Christianity is the fellowship of gods. For those who don't know. Things have changed. Watch and see us take over the earth. Though for now, it may not appear to be so, relax, precept must be upon precept. The revelation knowledge of the believers' identity must completely be installed in the soul-faculty for this course we effectually labour in teaching.

MIRROR 7.8
The Knowledge Of This Glory

The voice of him that crieth in the wilderness, Prepare ye the way of the LORD, make straight in the desert a highway for our God. Every valley shall be exalted, and every mountain

> and hill shall be made low: and the crooked shall be made straight, and the rough places plain: And the glory of the LORD shall be revealed, and all flesh shall see it together: for the mouth of the LORD hath spoken it" Isaiah 40:3-5.

> "As it is written in the book of the words of Esaias the prophet, saying, The voice of one crying in the wilderness, Prepare ye the way of the Lord, make his paths straight. Every valley shall be filled, and every mountain and hill shall be brought low, and the crooked shall be made straight, and the rough ways shall be made smooth; And all flesh shall see the salvation of God" Luke 3:4-6.

Compare both scriptures you find out that salvation is the glory Prophet Isaiah saw that would be revealed to all flesh. The glory of this latter house is salvation. Please don't mistake it for what you call end times moves.

> "The glory of this latter house shall be greater than of the former, saith the LORD of hosts: and in this place will I give peace, saith the LORD of hosts" Haggai 2:9.

The knowledge of this glory (salvation) is what will cover the earth. This is the knowledge of life and immortality revealed in the face of Jesus from within our spirit personality. Salvation captures the entire inheritance (called glory) of the believer in Christ. It is not a topic; it is God as the spirit personality of the man in Christ.

I call you blessed.

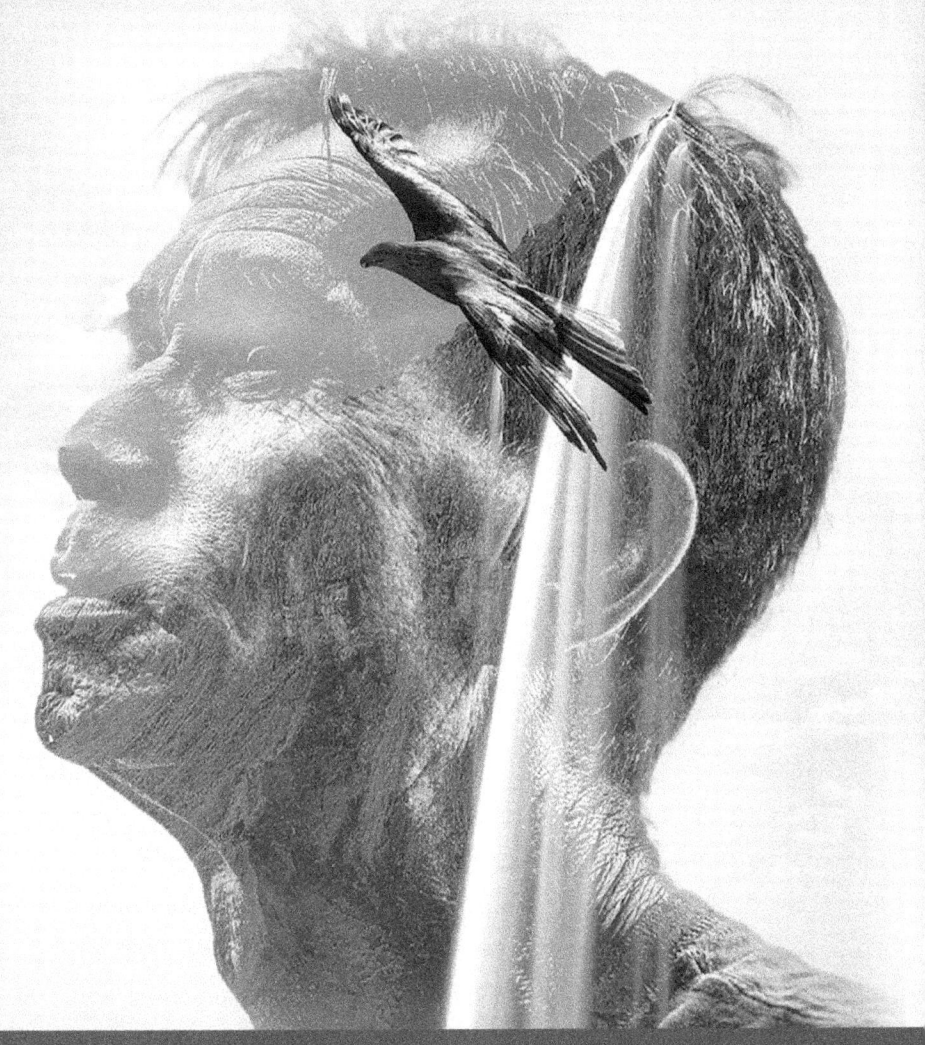

MIRROR EIGHT
TEACHING SERIES

IDENTITY SERIES - CODE 1

MIRROR 8.0
He Sees Us As He Is

The living person of the Son is our spirit's personality in Christ. God sees us precisely the way He sees the Son because both the Son (the sanctifier) and the believers (the sanctified) are one spirit. We are all Sons of God. God cannot speak outside of the Son. God cannot talk to you in the light of who you are not (your weaknesses).

Ministers learn.

Irrespective of the state of your soul and body, He addresses you in the light of who you are in your spirit's personality in Christ. So if a believer says that God spoke to him that he is foolish, know that's a lie. Even when God corrects a believer, He doesn't use derogatory words to address him. Righteousness in love is His rod of correction. He exposes the believer's heart to his spirit's nature in Him. Let's be instructed; this is serious.

The son is God speaking. When God speaks the primary goal is not to solve your temporary issues, those issues are merely side effects that are taken care of; please be clear on this. When God speaks, it is primarily to bring in view the face of the living Son, which is our spirit's personality. Ultimately, He intends to lead us to conform in our soul and body towards perfection.

MIRROR EIGHT

To most people, morality and ethical behavior is their yardstick to measure authentic Christian living, but God is after the breaking forth of divinity from within the saints, while the former is just side effect of the latter. The knowledge of God's glory is embodied in our spirit's personality.

> *"Now thanks be unto God, which always causeth us to triumph in Christ, and maketh manifest the savour of his knowledge by us in every place"* 2 Corinthians 2:14.

If we must penetrate every place (all spheres of society), it must be by the knowledge of our spirit's personality. This is how God will spread the fragrance of His person in every sphere of life.

MIRROR 8.1
Revelation Of Truth Are To Build The Body

Ministers, understand that revelation of truth are to build the brethren and never to prove a point. Settle this in your heart; no man called you to do what you are doing. For he who called you is the Lord and pleasing Him should be your one desire in ministry. Moreover, the Lord desires that His Body (the believers) is built and perfected in the complete revelation knowledge of their spirit's personality. This is why you must have a sense of responsibility while bringing forth the revelation of truth via teaching to the Body (the believers).

Your aim is not to have men praise or like you, but to please the Lord who sent you. Relax, don't border yourself with the validation of men. Just be in tune with the Lord. What will make your work stand the test of fire before the Lord is not the likes on your post or the praises and accolades of men you received. Delivering your responsibility based on the Lord's terms is all that matters and shall count.

Another thing to deal with is this. Have you heard people say I don't like to share revelation? Sometimes when I hear people say that am like are you serious? Are you the Lord of yourself? Such people are yet to understand that they are servants to the Lord as far as the work of ministry is concerned.

Let me clearly state this. You don't hoard revelation from the body (the believers) that you are privileged to access whether you have experienced it or not. Sharing it must be on the Lord's terms, not yours. The responsibility to ensure that it becomes an experience is a personal decision for all to make.

Note; although Paul touched certain depth in Christ, he never experienced everything he penned down. However, the revelation of the Master was through him to the body (the believers), which was not under his prerogative whether to share or not.

This is why many have been shut down from the flow of revelation because they don't know what is personal to them and what the Lord is generally speaking to (the believers) the body through them. The Lord had to rebuke me on this some months back.

MIRROR EIGHT

Every person is to run with the vision of God's revelation to the (the believers) body including the one through whom it came and the ones to whom it is given.

Dear ministers, we should never make light of this. Learn the wisdom of building the (the believers) body with the revelation of the truth on the Lord's prerogative. As ministers, we don't share revelation because we don't want to but because the Lord will have us restricted. This should be the attitude of a servant.

The fact that you have experienced and understood a particular revelation doesn't mean it is a go-ahead to share. No sir, it should be the Lord leading you. It should have nothing to do with what you like or dislike. As ministers, as far as the Lord's work is concerned, you are a servant, never forget that.

Don't forget that it is His Body and He is the one responsible to decide what to feed the Body with. A wise master builder is one that follows the leading of the Lord in the building.

MIRROR 8.2
Believers Are Already In Heaven

This verse in John 13 reveals that Jesus came to the full knowledge of His immortal personality as God. Also, He knew He was not returning to heaven after His assignment. He was returning to God; meaning He was returning to His estate as God ever before eternity came into being.

> *"Jesus, knowing (fully aware) that the Father had put everything into His hands, and that He had come from God and was [now] returning to God" John 13:3 (AMP).*

I went to a very populated denomination and realised that their goal in ministry is to make heaven. Dear believer, you are already in heaven. Christ is your heaven. You must be FULLY AWARE of what you became at new birth. This is the step towards exploring your immortal personality in Christ. It takes the revelation knowledge of your spirit's nature to be functional as God.

How can heaven be your goal when the reality of your life essence is beyond the heavens? Alternatively, don't you know that you are an uncreated spirit personality? Making "going to heaven" your goal is an assault on your Father. Your heaven is the Christ within you. To function in this heaven, you need the revelation knowledge of your immortal spirit's personality.

MIRROR 8.3

Revelation Knowledge Of Your Spirit Personality

The revelation knowledge of your spirit's personality is all you need to walk victoriously above death, sicknesses, and addictions. Dwell enough on the reality of your

MIRROR EIGHT

immortal personality through contemplative communion and see divinity break out from within you.

You must set the face of your spirit's personality always before your soul, no matter what you are doing or where you are. Set it before your soul whether you are in the toilet or living room. Set it before your soul while walking on the road. Set it before your soul while at work. Set it before your soul while with friends, acquaintances, and families. Also, while praying, set it before your soul, because you can be praying and yet not have the face of your immortal personality in view.

The revelation knowledge of your immortal spirit's personality is not just a sermon but teaching that must be woven into your daily life such that it becomes the tapestry of your life.

Some days ago at my place of work, someone asked me, why am I getting so obsessed with my spirit's personality, identity, and immortality? I said that's my life, and has become my obsession. It has taken over my subconscious mind.

For me, I have found the truth (life and immortality), and no matter what it costs me, I will go where ever I can have it spoken to me over and over again until my thinking process is completely altered by it. This is how seriously embracing this truth is.

Bring any knowledge to me other than the revelation knowledge of my spirit's personality even if you offer it for free, I won't buy into it. However, let it be the knowledge of the truth of my spirit's personality with a price tag; it is worth giving up everything for.

I am not one of those people seeking to be vast in all kinds of things. My head is not meant to accumulate facts, but my life desire is to come to the knowledge of the truth and live by it, that's all that counts and matters to me.

Like I have always said, this gospel is no man's opinion. It is the revelation of RIGHTEOUSNESS. No one is a spectator. You too can begin to sound this trumpet today because it is the song for everyone to sing and experience.

MIRROR 8.4

What Is A Sin?

Putting on the new man means renewing the mind with the revelation knowledge of your spirit's personality. God has begotten you in righteousness and true holiness. Holiness is the very nature of your being. You are righteousness. Perfecting holiness in our soul is not possible if we don't first recognize and acknowledge the finished work of God, which is our spirit's nature. Holiness in conduct, thoughts, and actions are expressions of the inward revelation knowledge of your spirit's personality as righteousness.

It is impossible for sin consciousness to produce a holy living. We must teach the believer the truth of his spirit's nature, which is Christ. Let your teaching be a mirror by which the believer beholds himself as perfect and complete in Christ. Don't allow yourself to be used by the devil to sponsor a sense of condemnation in the believer.

As far as the believer is concerned, sin is not his problem. Sin does not exist (it is dead) in the believer. He that was made sin is the same that died. Sin was crucified on the Cross.

What is Sin?

Sin is the perverted nature of a cherubic life, which Adam inherited when he identified with the fallen cherub (the devil) through disobedience to God's instructions. If we should take our time to understand this definition of sin, certain areas of contention will be taking care of. However, this is different from sin as an act.

Jesus wasn't crucified to resolve the problem of sin as an act but to eternally deal with sin as a nature. Sin as a nature cannot be forgiven; it can only be extinguished (abolished and destroyed). This was what Jesus did in His crucifixion. So, sin as a nature is eternally destroyed in the believer. Sin is not the problem of the believer forever.

Does the believer err? Yes, of course, believers sometimes err and commit the act of sin, but this is mainly because we have not had our mind renewed enough with the revelation knowledge of our spirit's nature, which is perfect, pure, holy, complete and blameless forever. So the believer's problem is an unrenewed mind.

Preaching hellfire and condemnation is not the solution to this problem. The answer is teaching believers the truth of their immortal spirit's personality. The believer has been forever saved and perfected. No matter how unrenewed his soul is, he cannot become unsaved again. He has passed from death to life. The gap between death and life is the sin nature, which Jesus has annihilated and eradicated or better still, put away by the sacrifice of Himself once and for all.

The believer is life now. He is incapable of eternal condemnation; meaning that his righteousness nature cannot become sin nature again. Don't get me wrong, please. A believer who continues in the act of sin is carnal and needs to be taught the truth of grace. Grace condemns you like a love slave to act in alignment with your spirit's nature. It is demeaning to live contrarily of who you are.

Dear believer, understand that grace is the therapy for an unrenewed mind. Nobody is accurately taught grace and goes ahead to live carelessly. Check out these verses of scripture.

> *"For the love of Christ constraineth us; because we thus judge, that if one died for all, then were all dead: And that he died for all, that they which live should not henceforth live unto themselves, but unto him which died for them, and rose again" 2 Corinthians 5:14-15.*

Yes, there is such thing as the daily consecration of the believer to the Lord we daily separate ourselves from worldly influence and corruption in other to please the LORD.

MIRROR EIGHT

- Grace is a holy lust to live for Jesus alone
- Grace enslaves you in love to live for Him
- Grace is the Father mesmerizing us with love such that we uncontrollably lust after Him.

This is the Gospel!

MIRROR 8.5
The Believer Is God Himself

All the dimensions within the realm of the Godhead are mapped into the believer's spirit's nature. He is a portal through which eternal transactions take place.

The believer is God Himself as his life essence; his spirit is God's nature of immortality.

- He is life
- He is immortal
- He is righteousness
- He is the new creation
- He is the embodiment of existence
- He is self-existing his "self" Christ

- He is an uncreated being beyond the globe of the ever-expanding eternity

The believer does not go to places outside of him because within him are all the places in God. He is the very substance (glory) resident in all the places within his being! This is the glory of his life.

Contrary to popular opinion, do you think any celestial being is capable of being a custodian of our inheritance? What do you think is your inheritance? Your inheritance is the glory that only God is capable of covering until it is fully manifested. God is the custodian of your inheritance, which is the full manifest glory of His life's essence.

It is beyond what any created spirit being can handle. Celestial beings cannot keep custody of that glory; your inheritance is beyond what they can keep custody of. They desire to look into it. Meaning; they wish to experience what is beyond their reach, which has now been made available to the man in Christ. Not because God is hiding it from them, but because their makeup is incapable of housing such glory. Contrary to some, cherub cannot "guard" the glory of God's life. The glory of God is sustaining them!

Let me simply put it. Your inheritance is that which excludes God from the class of His creation. It is called eternal life. You were not created; God begot you. You are in the class of God. We don't yet know the riches of the glory of eternal life in the saints. Words are too limited to articulate it.

Your inheritance is God Himself as your life's essence.

MIRROR EIGHT

MIRROR 8.6
Seeing Believers In The Light Of Who They Are

The moment you begin to see believers in the light of who they are in their spirit's personality, love and honour for them will naturally flow from you to them.

Now question.

If a man who cannot see himself in the light of who he is in Christ, how can he appreciate other believers like himself?

A man's expression is based on the revelation knowledge he has of himself. Please teach believers who they are. God didn't send you to point them to their weaknesses but to their identity in Christ, whom they became at the new birth.

MIRROR 8.7
We Are In The Father

The work of atonement wasn't complete with the resurrection of Jesus Christ. The process was completed in His first ascension immediately He arose from the dead to present Himself to the Father in the Holy of Holies. It was after this that redemption could be possible. That was how the new and living was initiated. This is what it means for Jesus to be the way; He describes Himself as the atonement. It was on this ground that He obtained the inheritance of eternal life as a man for man. This was the glory of life that followed. Himself as the truth and life describes His estate of glory after His death and resurrection. What a glory to behold!

All that Jesus said in John 14 prophetically described His work of redemption as the way and the glory of life that should follow.

In the Father's house; that was God as the habitation of Himself. The mansions are the living realities of glory within the habitation of Himself. The Father dwells in light, yet Himself is the light. (It's a Mystery).

Some people said the house is the Church that's not so correct because the Church was not yet born at the time Jesus said in my Father's house. Others said it is a physical building that's certainly not it. However, hallelujah the Church is now the dwelling-house of God.

However, it is essential that we put some things into perspective for us to get a clear picture. We are together now in the father. Jesus as the way brought us to the Father. As believers we don't have to go through "Jesus" as a medium to talk to the Father we are now in the Father. This is why we don't pray "through" the name of Jesus but in the name of Jesus. In the name of Jesus describes the living Christ in whom the union between God and man had taken place. This is the believers' authority. It is in the name we talk to God directly without any interface.

It is an assault on redemption when ministers begin to act as a medium through which the saints reach their Father even Jesus didn't make Himself a medium. For a believer to petition the Father through the anointing of a bishop, a pastor, a prophet, a daddy, a mummy, a GO and so forth, is to deny the truth of redemption. When we say the God of the apostle that answer us by fire the Father cries in His heart.

However, thank God for love. He will never allow us to wallow in ignorance for life. That's why truth is opening up. Moreover, with the Father's desire is to reach out in love, we sound the trumpet of truth. In Christ Jesus, we are forever in God's presence.

We cover the earth.

I love Jesus!

MIRROR 8.8
A Believer Is An Ever Ascending Fragrance Of Worship

The believer is an ever-ascending fragrance of worship. Worship is a reality beyond earthly words. It is an expression of the believer's life's essence to the Father. Learning to live and see ourselves from our spirit's personality is eternal worship to the Father.

Someone asked me why I am so selective with songs. I said, I only sing songs that capture my spirit's personality in Christ because that's the way the new creation man worships. The heart of worship is an unveiled heart. We are not moved by the "good voice" that cannot voice out the truth of redemption.

Someone said if we are to sing songs based on this reality, many songs will not pass the mark. Yes, that's because most people are skillful and passionate about singing without understanding what was wrought in redemption.

Moreover, people are more psychologically inclined to sound, so they don't border to examine songs in the light of redemption. Some call it spirit sound, no matter how they spiritualize it, we know is just emotionalism.

The new creation man is an embodiment of sound. He is the sound of God. He is an eternal melody in the heart of the Father and the song in the Father's lips.

The Father is more interested in the sound you generate from within your spirit's personality because that is the melody in His heart. If you cannot hear the song (your spirit's personality) your Father is singing to you, surely, you cannot sing back to Him. If you cannot behold the revelation knowledge of your spirit's personality the Father is showing you, you cannot sing to Him.

Your singing to the Father is an expression of sight (revelation), so I can rate the level of your sight by the songs you sing. The

MIRROR EIGHT

revelation of your spirit's personality is key to unlocking the sound the Father desires to hear from you.

MIRROR 8.9

Salvation Is Man's Elevation

Dear believer, understand that salvation is more of man's elevation than restoration. You were not only restored in right standing with God; you became one life with the Godhead. You were not restored to the position of the first Adam as a living soul spirit being before his fall but elevated to be a life-giving spirit.

In salvation, God did not only redeem man from sin much more, But He also exalted man into the class of Himself as an immortal spirit. The Godhead has one life

- The Godhead has one nature
- That one nature is God as the Father
- That one nature is God as the Son
- That one nature is God as the Holy Ghost
- That one nature is God as the Believer in Christ

Why is one of the members of the Godhead called Father? Some people have said is because He is the creator or originator of all things. That couldn't have been true because the Son and the Holy Ghost are as much the creator or originator of all things as the Father. So that wasn't the reason why God as the Father was called Father. Selah!

Do you know that when the Godhead lived alone, before they created anything, none of the members was called the "name" Father, Son or the Holy Spirit? They were equally and indivisibly one God. The concept of trinity never existed.

The idea of God as the Father, God as the Son, and God has the Holy Spirit came into being with the conception of redemption plan for man. Their separation was by their unique functions, as far as redemption was concerned. Redemption has always been the eternal melody in God's heart even before creation. All of God went into redemption in other to bring man into that one life and one nature with Him.

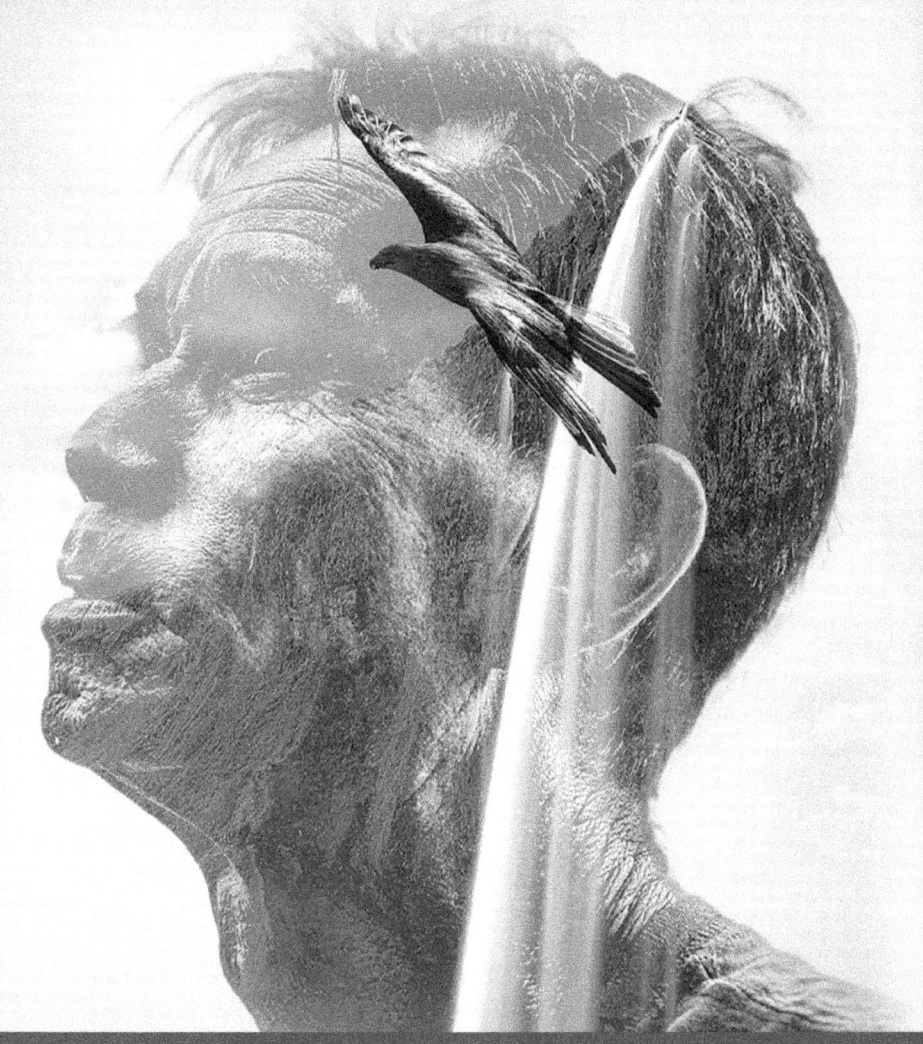

MIRROR NINE
TEACHING SERIES

IDENTITY SERIES - CODE 1

MIRROR 9.0

Redemption

Jesus said unto them, If God were your Father, ye would love me: for I proceeded forth and came from God; neither came I of myself, but he sent me" John 8:42.

"No man(No being) hath seen God at any time; the only begotten Son, which is in the bosom of the Father(within the father), he hath declared him" John 1:18.

"I came forth from the Father, and am come into the world: again, I leave the world, and go to the Father" John 16:28.

"Jesus knowing that the Father had given all things into his hands and that he was come from God, and went to God" John 13:3.

"But when the Comforter comes, whom I will send unto you from the Father, even the Spirit of truth, which proceedeth from the Father, he shall testify of me" John 15:26.

"Howbeit when he, the Spirit of truth, is come, he will guide you into all truth: "for he shall not speak of himself"; but whatsoever he shall hear, that shall he speak, and he will shew you things to come" John 16:13.

In the scriptures above can you see the Son saying He was sent from the Father (came out from the Father)? Do you also notice the Son saying "I will send" unto you the Spirit from the Father (who came out of the father too)? Both God as the Son and God as the Holy Ghost proceeded from God as the Father.

MIRROR NINE

There wouldn't have been God as the Father if God didn't decide to become a Son and also God coming forth out of Himself (father) as the Holy Ghost were all for the purpose of redemption. Redemption was the one will for which they had a defined role in function. Redemption reveals the humility and the total submission to one another in the indivisible union of the Godhead.

God coming forth as the Holy Ghost means that God became the messenger under the testament of the Son. The Holy Ghost is the Spirit of Truth saddled with the responsibility to bear witness to the truth. The truth is the testament of the Son. The Holy Ghost who is the Spirit of truth is the messenger of the message. He is not the message. This is why Jesus said that the comforter whom He will send will "not" speak of Himself but will testify of Me. Can you see that in your Bible?

As the messenger, He only doesn't bear witness to the truth, He is the only one capable of bringing us into experiencing the truth. This testament of the Son called truth is the immortal reality of the Godhead captured in redemption, which is now available to man. Angels cannot teach you the truth. They are the ones to learn the truth from us.

The revelation knowledge of the humility and submission in the Godhead humbles my heart. Each of them sees it as glory and honour to serve one another in total submission. Imagine one choose to be born as a Son to do the will of the Father, and the other decided to be the servant under the testament of the risen Son. Awesome!

The most spectacular character of the Godhead is servanthood. Believers understand that serving one another in love is the very nature of our Father. The unity of the faith we are to come into mirrors this reality in the Godhead.

The Holy Ghost has a defined task which is to bring us into truth in all the immortal realm of God, as captured under the testament of the Son. It is unfortunate that a lot of believers think that all that the Holy Ghost is here to do is just for the manifestations of power. While some others believe the Holy Ghost is here to rain down fire to kill witches and wizards.

The Holy Ghost is the Spirit that baptises us into all truth and experientially bringing us into the reality of our immortal identity in God.

This is why the word fellowship is used in association with Him because fellowship describes how He brings us into the experiences of what had been wrought in the testament (grace) of the son as a result of God's love.

MIRROR 9.1
What Is Light?

God has reproved by exposing to light! It is in the light that the true nature of a thing is revealed. It is light that makes manifest.

> *"But all things that are reproved are made manifest by the light: for whatsoever doth make manifest is light"* Ephesians 5:13.

What Is Light?

Light is the revelation knowledge of the truth. The Spirit of truth reproved the world of sin by exposing to light the true nature of sin. Truly, we know what sin is today because it has been exposed to light by the Holy Ghost. He had reproved the believer by exposing him to righteousness (his nature); this is how we came into the revelation knowledge of righteousness.

Satan's total defeat (judgment) had been exposed to light by the revealed truth of the Holy Ghost. This is what Jesus meant here.

> *"Nevertheless I tell you the truth; it is expedient for you that I go away: for if I go not away, the Comforter will not come unto you; but if I depart, I will send him unto you. And when he comes, he will(as at then he has not) reprove the world of sin, and of righteousness, and of judgment: Of sin, because they believe not me; Of righteousness, because I go to my father; and ye see me no more; Of judgment, because the prince of this world is judged"* John 16:7-11.

The Holy Ghost had already reproved, and this reprove is the revelation of truth revealed in the epistles about what sin is, the true nature of righteousness and how satan has been judged and defeated. These are all revealed in the epistles of Paul.

> *I explained in one of my write up what Jesus meant when He said righteousness "because" I go to my Father and ye see me not." It was also captured in chapter 14 of John.*

Jesus' going to the Father (Jesus as the way) described the redemptive work of atonement which was completed not when He resurrected, but when He first ascended to present Himself before the Father. It was on this account we were declared righteous and made righteousness.

> *"Jesus saith unto her, touch me not; for I am not yet ascended to my father" John 20:17.*

People have used that (John 16:8) to say the Holy Ghost reproves the believer of sin that's not true but does the Holy Ghost reproves a believer when he does wrong, yes, but He reproves him by exposing him to the already revealed righteousness; He makes the believer see himself in the light of truth.

MIRROR 9.2
A Believers Nature Is The God-Life

Dear believer, understand that your very nature is the God-life; you have become one immortal spirit with God. The testimony of the new testament in the living

MIRROR NINE

Christ is that "we have become partakers of the divine nature."

> *"Whereby are given unto us exceeding great and precious promises: that by these ye might be partakers of the divine nature, having escaped the corruption that is in the world through lust" 2 Peter 1:4.*

The divine nature is the complete divinity of the Godhead embodied in Christ, which we have come to share together! THIS IS RIGHTEOUSNESS. God is fully complete in us. We are His Holy of Holies where He fully resides in His totality in glory.

Contrary to some opinion. The new creation man doesn't enter God's courts. What we call the courts of God are living realities of His government that issues out from within the believer immortal being. The believer doesn't approach. He is not coming to God's throne. Some people think that's what this place in the book of Hebrew was talking about. That's not it!

> *"Let us, therefore, come boldly unto the throne of grace, that we may obtain mercy, and find grace to help in time of need" Hebrews 4:16.*

The throne of grace is not a chair where God sits. Don't forget the writer was talking to the Jewish Christians who at a time went into Judaism (they were Christians yet practicing works)

That's why the message of the book of Hebrew apart from the depth of truth revealed about the priesthood of Christ was to point those believers to the finished work of Christ as the ONLY FAITH for salvation. Dear believer, with this understanding study the book again some point will become more apparent to you.

So what the writer meant by the throne of grace (which is figurative) is the PROVISION OF REDEMPTION, coming boldly before the throne of grace means taking advantage of the finished work (provision) in redemption. Our language is limited indeed to explain spiritual realities.

God's throne is His sovereign DOMINION over all things created, which now defines your reality as an immortal spirit. His throne is the resurrection power at work in you. We are yet to scratch 1% of resurrection power within us. This is why we cannot ignore the revelation knowledge of who we are because it is how we gain stature in the path of spiritual progress.

What Then Is Stature?

It is to experientially come into the complete revelation knowledge (epignosis) of your spirit's nature. (your spirit's nature is divinity). The face of Yahweh is the Christ reality that you became in your spirit's nature. This is why we don't seek the face of God (that's for old testament forks) we are the bearer of His face we carry His face wherever we go. The face of God is an immortal reality within our being.

MIRROR NINE

MIRROR 9.3
Christ Became As A Man For Man At Resurrection

We were the joy that was set before Him when He went through the agony of the cross. All that Jesus became in the resurrection is a man for man. God's only reward from redemption are the many sons who have become one with His life. Outside of this, there was nothing He gained in return.

> *"And now, O Father, glorify thou me with thine own self with the glory which I had with thee before the world was"* John 17:5.

Jesus could not be more glorified with the glory He has always had as God before anything created.

- He was the first new creation man
- He received this glory now as a man for man
- Jesus was glorified not as God but as a man
- You are what Jesus became at the resurrection
- He was the first to be made the righteousness of God

We know that when Jesus was on earth his nature WASN'T RIGHTEOUSNESS. He only had an INNOCENT nature of a living soul spirit being like the first Adam before His fall. He wasn't eternal life in His nature. He was alive to God. Relax and think about that.

If His nature was RIGHTEOUSNESS while He was on earth there was no way possible; He could have been MADE sin. Righteousness nature which is eternal life or immortal life is incapable of becoming sin. An innocent nature is capable of corruption. It was possible for Jesus to have been corrupted if He had not endured all the temptation against Him.

> *"For we have not an high priest which cannot be touched with the feeling of our infirmities; but was in all points tempted like as we are, yet without sin" Hebrews 4:15.*

He was without sin, having been tempted not because He was God but because He endured the process. Take your time and Understand this truth. This is why as a life-given spirit that you are (as righteousness) still in a mortal body the devil is not tempting in other to corrupt your nature. He knows you have become incapable of corruption. His only purpose of attack through ignorance is to make you function less of who you are, but he can never pervert who you are. Selah!

Sin is incapable of corrupting who you are as righteousness. God's divine nature that we are partakers of is not innocent, by that I mean God's divine nature is not merely without sin, but righteousness. The nature of angels in their order of life is innocent (without sin) but not righteousness. That is why they are also capable of corruption; in other words; they are not immortals and incorruptible beings.

What we call sin is a nature that produces sinful acts. The opposite of sin nature is not righteousness nature but an innocent nature. This should be clear to you.

Righteousness nature is opposite to nothingness. It is in the class of its own. If righteousness nature should enter hell, hell will go out of extinction. Nothing of death can stand or overcome it. This is what Jesus became after the resurrection. So I can now say that while Jesus was on earth, He wasn't the righteousness of God. He was innocent as the first Adam before his fall. Sin was not in Him, but He was capable of sinning. This was the possibility of Him being made sin that we might become the righteousness of God in Him.

As righteousness of God, we don't have that potential in us. As believers born of God, we are forever incapable of sin. God did so much in redemption than the physical senses can comprehend. He brought man into that glory of immortal life, which was exclusive to the Godhead.

The Father will patiently see to it that the saints are perfected (come into stature) of the full capacity of the divine life in knowledge. God's desire is for us to function in the full capacity of the divine life which can only be achieved through the revelation knowledge of life and immortality.

IDENTITY SERIES - CODE 1

MIRROR 9.4

The Revelation Knowledge Of Your Spirit's Personality

The revelation knowledge of your spirit's personality as "I am," disengages the genetic code of time in the mortal reality within your soul faculty. Your spirit's personality is the "ever-present one;" as an immortal being you have no past, and you have no future. You are ageless in your spirit's nature. All ages are compressed into your present. You are already in the age or in the world to come. However, those who are bound and limited by time-consciousness, the age or the world to come, is still futuristic. They cannot comprehend their present reality. But to those who see from the lens of their immortal personality the age to come is a "now" reality.

"I am" means the ever-present one. God has no past and future. Everything consists in His presence. He neither has a birth date nor death date, so He doesn't have a particular day He celebrates those events. The reality of "I am" is locked up in the DNA of God, within our spirit's nature.

If your birth date in the flesh is more real to your consciousness than the power of an endless life contained in your spirit's personality, it will result in mortal experience. Selah!

satan knows this; that's why he always arrange events in our lives that always keep us alive in that consciousness.

MIRROR NINE

You must be daring enough not to acknowledge certain events in other to keep the sanctity of your soul to behold eternal reality. However, don't be critical with others, if they act otherwise.

May our eyes be enlightened enough to see this reality. It is always a normal thing for some to see you as an extremist, but love them in return and keep the reality in view.

If they are still alive, they will eventually come to see and agree with what you have seen days ahead of them. Some persons only need to be given some time to come to terms with you, eventually. Allow them to enjoy the privilege of sustaining a different position from you. But still, love each other nonetheless, and don't cast stones at each other. That's maturity.

Who are you? Answer: I am. The revelation knowledge of that answer will set you on another journey. Am just in love with you.

MIRROR 9.5

What Is The Truth?

Truth is the uncreated spirit personality that you became at new birth. You are what Jesus became at the resurrection. The revelation knowledge of this truth within the soul-faculty is what births eternal transformation. The revelation knowledge of this truth within your soul faculty is the basis for real discernment. A transformed soul discerns all things.

"And be not conformed to this world: but be ye transformed by the renewing of your mind, that ye may prove what is that good, and acceptable, and perfect, will of God" Romans 12:2.

The word "prove" means to discern or to try. It is not talking about the gift of discernment. The word "prove" was used in connection with a renewed mind; the word was also used here in the scripture below.

"Beloved, believe not every spirit, but PROVE the spirits whether they are of God: because many false prophets are gone out into the world" 1 John 4:1.

It is talking about the discernment that is as a result of a renewed mind. This kind of discernment is an expression of the nature of truth by which you now see through your soul. A man can have the gift of discernment but still be suffering carnality in his soul. A carnal mind is an unrenewed mind; it captures the knowledge of death in the soul faculty that informs the man's sight and actions.

An unrenewed mind is not just a veil in the heart. It is a distortion of pure streams. They affect our level of spiritual sight. When the revelation knowledge of your spirit's personality becomes your heart posture, you can discern all things

The mind of Christ is captured within your spirit's nature which is imported to your soul faculty via revealed truth. Fellowshipping with divine truth is romancing the personality of your spirit's nature in the Father.

Yes, that's what it means to gaze on the beauty of the Lord. It is communion with one's self in the Father. Your "self" is Christ

MIRROR NINE

"When Christ, [who is] our life, shall appear, then shall ye also appear with him in glory" Colossians 3:4.

- You are the glory of God
- You are the beauty of the LORD

Your soul is transformed to reflect the beauty of the Lord in your spirit's nature as you behold who you are in Christ.

It is wrong for the believer to repeat the words of John in his prayer to the Lord.

> *"He must increase, but I must decrease" John 3:30.*

Don't forget the "I" he said that must decrease is his unregenerated nature that is why he said in the following verse that;

> *"He that COMETH FROM ABOVE is above all: he that is of the earth is earthly, and speaketh of the earth: he that cometh from heaven is above all" John 3:31.*

You Are The One From Above. Your "I" Is Christ

This means that the unregenerated "I" has been put to death.

> *"I am crucified with Christ: nevertheless I live; yet not I, but Christ liveth in me: and the life which I now live in the flesh I live by the faith of the Son of God, who loved me, and gave himself for me" Galatians 2:20.*

You Are The "I" That Must Increase

This means that the revelation knowledge of your spirit's nature is gaining dominance in your soul faculty.

- You are one spirit with truth
- You are one with the anointing
- You must live from your "I" Selah!
- You are what Jesus became at the resurrection
- You cannot decrease because you are above all, you are one spirit with God

MIRROR 9.6
Subjecting The Stronghold Of The Soul

The revelation knowledge of your spirit's personality brings to subjection every stronghold in your soul. What many are yet to understand, especially the majority of ministers, is that the moment you deviate from the mirror principle of teaching, you end up enslaving God's people to a life of perpetual bondage.

To detect a problem in a believer's life or the Body of Christ at large is one thing, and to deal with that problem is a different thing entirely. Unfortunately, most people inadvertently exacerbate the problem by exalting it above the solutions. This approach eventually makes the believer becomes "problem conscious "and renders him helpless. If you do this, you are not a wise master builder.

MIRROR NINE

The issues in the soul of the believer are exposed to light through revelation knowledge, in such a way that he is empowered to walk above the challenges, without the sense of fear or condemnation. This is not about being careful; it is about the flow of divine life from within him.

As ministers, if we don't humbly submit to this wisdom of mirror principles of teaching, we will incapacitate the Body of Christ by our problems conscious way of teaching and doing ministry.

Understand that the ongoing work in the believer's life has a foundation to it. You don't teach the believer to put on the new man without first bringing him to the revelation knowledge of himself "as" the new man. The putting on of the new man is in the revealing of who they are in their being. Without this order, we will have a lot of incapacitated and weak believers in the Body of Christ. If you keep emphasizing weakness, you will ultimately produce weaklings.

If you are good at dissecting the works of the flesh but poor at presenting the truth of the spirit's life, know that your pew is full of crippled people than walking people. You are not called to preach the works of the flesh, but the works of the spirit of life in Christ Jesus. Teaching believers to walk above the works of the flesh is not in mere preaching. You need the revelation of your immortal personality in Christ.

> *"Now the works of the flesh are manifest, which are these; Adultery, fornication, uncleanness, lasciviousness" Galatians 5:19.*

This is our emphasis in what God has mandated us to do for the Body of Christ.

> *"And they that are Christ's have crucified the flesh with the affections and lusts" Galatians 5:24.*

This is the exposure that empowers the believer above the former. Everything in it has an order. It is arrogance to lift anything outside of its order. No one ever walks above the works of the flesh with the sense of fear or as though they are subject to them.

Hatred is not the believer's reality; it may be an issue in his soul but not his reality. It is the revelation knowledge of his reality that alters the condition of his soul. His reality is that" he is a love being." Preach this enough to him and see what happens next in his life.

The mirror principle of teaching is hidden in this verse.

> *"For ye were sometimes darkness, but now are ye light in the Lord: walk as children of light" Ephesians 5:8.*

"Ye are light" speaks of "being;" your spirit's nature. " Walk as light" speak of "doing;" the expression of your spirit's nature. The former is the foundation for the latter. If the revelation knowledge of your "being" has no SOLID HOLD on your heart, you will live a life of perpetual struggle. Be a wise builder.

The face of the spirit's nature is the mirror the soul should be beholding. This is the mirror principle. For those who sincerely want to build, embraces this way of teaching.

MIRROR NINE

MIRROR 9.7
A Believer Is Not Becoming A Son

Imagine separating yourself for weeks to fast and pray with a dedication to scriptures, focusing on this prayer point?

PRAYER FOCUS: "Holy Spirit enlighten my soul with the revelation knowledge of my spirit's nature in the immortal Christ that I may fully know myself in the light of what Jesus became at the resurrection."

I can assure you that you will come out of that spiritual exercise with a measure of change that words cannot articulate. Try and see what happens next.

Be Intentional With Growth

Dear believer, do you know that no created spirit being within eternity understands how the new birth took place within the believer? How God brought forth Himself in Christ is a mystery, unfathomed by celestial beings. Many still don't know that at the new birth experience God gave birth to the being of Himself. This new being called the believer carries the DNA of his Father God; he is God, the son of God the Father.

- One life
- One spirit
- One throne
- One nature and One righteousness

***"For in him dwelleth all the fulness of the Godhead bodily"
Colossians 2:9-10.***

You are complete in him, which is the head of all principality and power. "To be complete in Him" means you have the full structure of the Godhead embodied within your spirit's nature like Jesus. The only difference is that Jesus as a man embodied it both in stature (knowledge) and life essence (nature).

Coming into the stature (knowledge) of the Godhead is the believer's only journey. This is what Paul by the spirit captured in this scripture.

"Till we all come in the unity of the faith, and of the knowledge of the Son of God, unto a perfect man, unto the measure of the stature of the fullness of Christ" Ephesians 4:13.

Notice something here: You are not coming to "be" son of God but to the "KNOWLEDGE" of the son of God. You are not coming into the fullness of Christ but to the "STATURE" of the fullness of Christ.

It is coming into the complete revelation knowledge of who you are, experientially. That is why anybody not teaching you who you are is "mortgaging your destiny for a bowl of meal." I believe you are clear on that. Now you are the holy of holies indwelling the Godhead. If anybody tells you that you need an "atmospheric portal" to connect to God, that's derogatory to the believer. Tell that person that you are the very atmospheric portal." God is nowhere else outside of you. This is why our various meetings as believers are synergies of life, not one person's celebrity movement.

MIRROR NINE

Christianity is the fellowship of gods in pure love and total submission to one another. Not a religion of dead activities (veils) that have made slaves out of true-born sons of the most high, but they shall continue no further the KNOWLEDGE of life and immortality is here to swallow and expose every veil and dishonest counsels in men's heart.

This is why when they cast stone, we cast love because we know that's the message working. The revelation knowledge of the spirit's nature is the mechanism by which we install life in our soul faculty. It is by the revelation of this truth we BUILD the body. Do you know what happened at new birth?

MIRROR 9.8
The Promise Of Abraham Is Redemption

The blessing of Abraham as a promise was redemption or the new birth fulfilled in Christ. He was declared righteous by faith without works in the hope of the new birth (note he wasn't made righteousness as at then) after the "Promised Seed" was glorified in His ascension.

It was on this ground that the "promised Spirit" captured in the prophecy of Joel (Joel 2:28) was released to facilitate the "Promised Seed" as a living experience of those in hope by faith, which is the new birth.

> *"Therefore being by the right hand of God exalted, and having received of the Father the promise of the Holy Ghost, he hath shed forth this (poured out), which ye now see and hear"* Acts 2:33.

The reason why Jesus asked the disciples to wait in Jerusalem for the promise of the Father, which was the "Promised Spirit," was because of regeneration. This was to be the result of the Holy Ghost baptism Jesus spoke about.

> *"For John truly baptized with water; but ye shall be baptized with the Holy Ghost not many days hence"* Acts 1:5.

What Was John's Baptism?

John's baptism was the baptism of repentance in the hope of Him that was to come which is Christ. But the Holy Ghost baptism was the experience of that hope, who is Christ as a living person in the believer. This is the new birth.

The Holy Ghost Was Not The Promise

The promise was Christ, but the Holy Ghost is the promised Spirit that makes the promise who is the resurrected Christ a living experience. This was what Jesus meant by the Holy Ghost baptism. He is the Spirit of promise that makes the promise a living experience.

This living experience is the power that is captured in Acts chapter 1 that the disciples would receive. It is not the power to cast out devils. The disciples had at some point cast out devils before Jesus died and resurrected. That power is the inherent living reality of the person that now indwells them.

MIRROR NINE

The new tongue was evidence of the reality that had taken place within them. Now, that evidence was a "sign" to them without, that God has fulfilled His promise as spoken by Prophet Joel.

For this reason, there are a set of believers who may not speak in tongues, yet it does not change the fact that they are believers. They can still cast out devils and demonstrate power. But every Christian should speak with tongues. Having this experience as a believer is essential. However, that is not proof that they are believers. For example, some believers started speaking in tongues instantaneously after the new birth, others begin speaking in tongues five years after, some don't even get to speak till they pass out of this life. That does not change the fact of what had taken place in them at the new birth.

What we call the spirit within and the spirit upon are not necessarily two different things just that the latter is just the overwhelming of that who is within. I know some may argue that the disciples got born again before Acts Chapter 2 because of what Jesus said in John Chapter 20.

> *"And when he had said this, he breathed on [them italicized], and saith unto them, Receive ye the Holy Ghost" John 20:22.*

Jesus spoke concerning what was going to happen after that. He prepared their hearts by telling them to receive, which is the Greek word "lambano." It means to take hold of. He kindled their expectation.

Do you realise that Thomas was not there with them when He said that? So, if they were indeed born again does that mean

Thomas missed it? Because there was no account of Jesus repeating what He said in John 20:22 to Thomas until they assembled together in Acts Chapter 1.

Please understand the way Jesus speaks. Sometimes He makes future reality a fulfilled present expectation. Before Jesus died and resurrected, sometimes He would say He gives eternal life. We know Jesus could not give anyone eternal life in the days of His flesh because eternal life is Himself as the life-giving Spirit indwelling in a man by the baptism of the Holy Ghost.

The r e surrected p o wer w ithin y ou i s y our s p irit's n a ture. I t i s Christ, as a living reality in you. That is the proof of the new birth.

You are blessed.

MIRROR 9.9

What Did Jesus Take Away At Redemption?

Jesus "took away" the sin of the "world" not the sin of the new creation man, why? Because the new creation man has never sinned once. We never existed before. So to say a believer has been delivered from sin is truth at a level and to say the believer is not the one who has been delivered from sin is another truth at another level.

How could the you who never existed before have been delivered from sin? What is the record that you have sinned before?

Think about that.

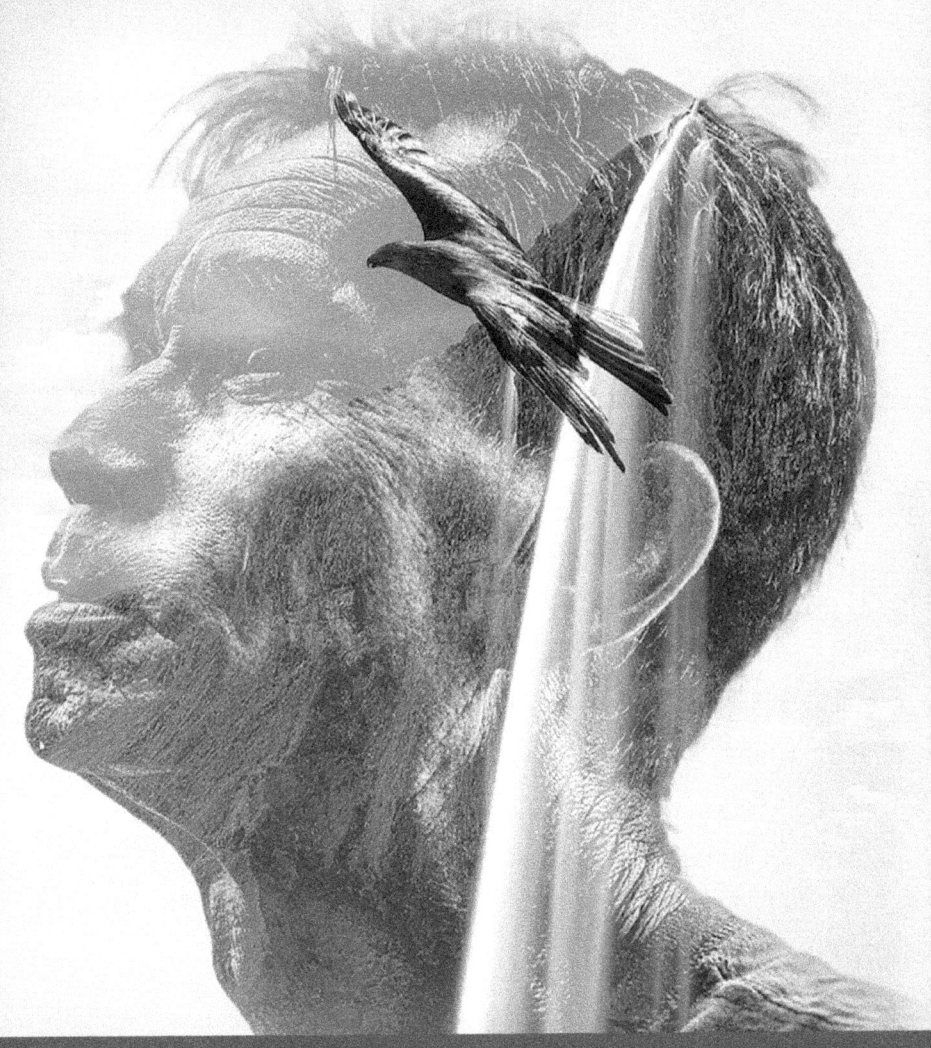

MIRROR TEN
TEACHING SERIES

IDENTITY SERIES - CODE 1

MIRROR 10.0

Yielding Yourself

Yielding yourself as one that is alive to God, captures the revelation knowledge of your spirit's personality as righteousness, which has become the heart posture of the soul. In other words, it has become a mindset.

Paul by the spirit was speaking in Romans 12:1 said; *"present your bodies a living sacrifice, holy and acceptable (pleasing) to the Lord."* The word "present" has the same meaning as the word "yield" as used in Romans 6:16. And also verses 2 of Romans 12, has a strong connection with verse 1, which is the subject.

Yielding ourselves or our bodies as alive to God means the setting apart (holy) of the body, as a result of a transformed soul, through the revelation knowledge of our spirit's nature as righteousness.

A renewed mind is the heart posture or the mechanism by which our bodies are set apart (holy and pleasing to God. It is the reality of your spirit's nature finding expression on your body through an altered soul condition (renewed mind). This is the meaning of perfecting holiness is the fear of God.

> *"Having, therefore, these promises, dearly beloved, let us cleanse ourselves from all filthiness of the flesh and spirit(note not your spirit nature but the soul or heart), perfecting holiness in the fear of God"* 2 Corinthians 7:1.

MIRROR TEN

"Filthiness of the flesh and spirit" means the works of the flesh in the soul.

- Your spirit's nature is holy
- You are forever blameless
- You are righteousness

The word "spirit" in that verse describes a robust state of the soul in connection with the filthiness of the flesh.

Now presenting your body as a living sacrifice, holy and pleasing to the Lord means setting your body apart as a conduit to express the reality of the spirit's life (righteousness) through a transformed soul condition. This is what it means to glorify God in your body and in your spirit.

> *"For ye are bought with a price: therefore glorify God in your body, and in your spirit, which are God's" 1 Corinthians 6:20.*

The glorifying God here in the context of the chapter is using the body for the Lord, not for fornication as rightly stated, but as an instrument of expression. That verse is saying we should glorify God in the spirit through the body, meaning using the body as an instrument for expressing the spirit-life, which is righteousness. But the mechanism by which such reality happens is the renewed mind.

IDENTITY SERIES - CODE 1

MIRROR 10.1

The New Creation Man Cannot Sin

The new creation man is God as man's spirit personality in Christ, who has never sinned before. Can God sin or has He sinned before?

Question!

Can the new creation man sin?

Answer!

No, sir! The new creation man doesn't have any of such potential in his DNA.

- He is life
- He is holiness
- He is righteousness

The new creation man CANNOT sin, and he had never sinned before because he never EXISTED BEFORE. He has no record of past life the record that we have of his origin is God; He is traced to God.

> *"Whoever has been born of God does not sin, for His seed remains in him; and HE CANNOT SIN, because he has been born of God"* 1John 3:9 (NKJV).

MIRROR TEN

The new creation man is the new man begotten from the womb of immortality (life). Believers are seen as those who have been delivered from sin, which is true in a sense but not the whole truth.

If you are a new creation man which means a new species or a new kind of being that never lived before, who was "you" that was delivered from sin? That "you" that was delivered from sin is the old man that was exchanged (not change) for the new man.

Please understand that "you" before the cross and "you" after the cross are two different persons. As a believer, the life you have is not the life of the old rugged Cross it is the resurrection life.

The old rugged cross was God's mechanism for putting an end to the old creation when He crucified sin in the body of Jesus. The "you" as a sinner and the sin as a nature within you were together crucified on the cross. Don't forget that we identified with sin in the first Adam and took on sin as a nature. We became one life with sin; this is what Jesus became in His spirit. He was made sin in His spirit. He became one life with sin, not just for man but as a man to end both the reality of the old creation man as a sinner (what He became) and the very sin within Him.

This is why we say that the believer is not a sinner saved from sin by grace, but he is righteousness who has never existed before as a sinner. Now, you as the new man has never known sin. If you should have any record, then your past, present and the future record is righteousness.

When you got born again, your soul and body didn't experience an automatic change. That is because the soul and the body are not the new creation man. This new creation man is you as a complete spirit being. Man is a full fledge spirit with a soul and body to function. But right now sin has worked on this soul and installed the knowledge of death into it and transform the body into a "dead state."

So the only place we have the knowledge and the experience of sin, which is death, is in our soul and body. Our spirit does not know what sin is because he has never experienced it before. The believer experiences the "act of sin" in his body because of his unrenewed mind. It is in this sense that we say the believer can commit the act of sin. It is his unrenewed mind finding expression, not his spirit's nature.

But as he gets awakened in his soul to the reality of who he is in his spirit's nature as righteousness, he unlearns the ways of death constituted into his soul as knowledge thereby reconfiguring the state of the body to live beyond death.

MIRROR 10.3
Your Inborn Personality

Wherefore lay apart all filthiness and superfluity of naughtiness, and RECEIVE with meekness the ENGRAFTED WORD, which is able to save your souls" James 1:21.

MIRROR TEN

> "But be ye DOERS OF THE WORD, and not hearers only, deceiving your own selves" James 1:22.
>
> "For if any be a hearer of the word and not a doer, HE IS LIKE unto a man BEHOLDING his natural face in a glass" James 1:23.
>
> "For he beholdeth himself, AND GOETH HIS WAY, and straightway FORGETH what manner of man he was" James 1:24.
>
> "But whoso LOOKETH [BEHOLD] into the PERFECT LAW OF LIBERTY, and CONTINUETH therein, he BEING NOT a FORGETFUL hearer, but a doer of the work, this man shall be BLESSED in his deed" James 1:25.

James by the spirit captures the mechanism by which we prosper in the work of transforming our soul.

Dear believer, understand that the engrafted word or the implanted word of truth is your inborn spirit's personality that is the perfect law of liberty through which we facilitate salvation in our souls.

Our spirit's nature is the perfect law of God that the Father is currently writing in our heart.

> "This is the covenant that I will make with them after those days, saith the Lord, I will put my laws into their hearts, and in their minds will I write them" Hebrews 10:16.

What Are The Laws Of God?

The laws of God are the knowledge of life inscribed in our spirit's nature. The mind of Christ is the laws of God as complete knowledge of divinity contained within our spirit's personality.

What God is currently doing is that He is writing the mind of Christ in our soul faculty; this is what He is facilitating by the spirit through the mirror principle of teaching. This principle means that the face or the image of your spirit's nature is the true mirror your soul should continuously behold.

Your spirit's personality is Christ. Hence you don't expose your soul to any kind of knowledge other than the revelation knowledge of your spirit's personality.

> "The law of the LORD is perfect, CONVERTING the soul: the TESTIMONY of the LORD is sure, making WISE the simple" Psalm19: 7.

> "The statutes of the LORD are right, rejoicing the heart: the commandment of the LORD is pure, enlightening the eyes" Psalm19: 8.

The mind of Christ captured within our spirit's nature is what converts the soul. The word "converting" in the original language means to restore or reconfigure or to reprogram. This is what the salvation of the soul is all about. It is the reconfiguration of the soul to align with eternal life in knowledge.

Now, this reconfiguration takes place as a result of consistently sticking to the process. This is where many people miss it. The reprogramming of the soul is easy if people will realise that there is a template by which reconfiguration takes place, which is the perfect law of liberty contained in the believer's spirit's identity as righteousness.

MIRROR TEN

The testimony of the Lord is the finished work of God, which is our spirit's personality as righteousness. It is the testimony of the God-life within our being. The knowledge of this life is the perfect law of liberty that converts our soul.

James by the spirit gave us the template for this, he captures it as looking or beholding. What does it mean to behold?

To behold means to consistently set your heart on the revealed truth of your spirit's personality until that reality alters your heart's posture or the condition of your soul. The you that you see through revelation knowledge is your spirit's nature in Christ immortal.

The doers of the works are those who consistently and continuously look into who they are in their spirit's nature without departing from looking. So, the doing is in the looking, and as that order is maintained, the soul prospers, which eventually impacts on the actions or conduct of the believer.

As a preacher or teacher, you must humbly submit to the mirror principle of teaching. Don't join the excellent analysts out there. They are experts at dissecting and exalting negative habits and attitude in the believer's soul. This form of preaching renders the simple-hearted ones helpless. These preachers don't realise that it is the testimony of life that makes wise the simple.

Because of the present state of the believer's soul, there are issues upon issues we may know about. Even you that point out things that are wrong with others are not immune to such problems too.

What many don't know is that you don't have to be loud about an issue you discover with people before you can deal with them. It is in emphasising the perfection of the believer to the believer through teaching that the issues in the soul of the believer are dealt with. This is wisdom.

And to you my dearly beloved, your personal responsibility is to keep your heart in the purest and perfect revelation of who you are in your spirit's nature. So guard your heart jealously that nobody penetrates it with just any knowledge. You are the landlord of your heart to decide what stays in there. Open your heart to the knowledge that brings out your beauty within, because that is where your strength to function resides, not the knowledge of your issues.

Many have unknowingly partnered with an accusing spirit. They will make you continue to see the issues of the works of the flesh in your soul like hatred and never will once expose you to your true nature as a love being. Such people don't understand how the work of transformation takes place within. So, while you pray for them because a lot of them sincerely don't know about this immortal reality of the believer's spirit's nature. However, never expose your heart to their teaching so you don't become a victim.

There are others who are expert in dissecting the mystery of pride and exalt it and overtakes your soul than they expose you to the true light of life that humbles the heart, from such turn away. With the fear of pride comes the reality of pride, and through

MIRROR TEN

the teaching and the dissecting, fear is being imported into your heart. Unfortunately, this is the subtle thing they don't detect, and that's what birth its reality. This is why others will hear such they will begin to put up false humility, which they don't realize is another manifestation of pride. Let the revelation of who you are humble your heart not fear!

Let Me Quickly Address This

Such thing as don't call me Apostle, I am just Saint Omo are real nonsense. That's not humility. There are people without titles that are clothed with pride. If you were genuinely called as an Apostle, tell me what is wrong if people address you by that office. Titles have never made anyone proud. Pride is a posture of the heart facilitated by a kind of knowledge. But certainly, not the mind of Christ captured in your spirit's nature, which is what your heart should be exposed to.

Don't joke with teaching, through teaching spirits influence are released over your heart. Whether you agree with it or not, influence has been released into your heart by simply reading this write up. You will realise it later. Except that you are very sensitive to trap it and get rid of it immediately. However, I am very sure this write up has released a positive life-changing influence in your heart, which is always my desire before I teach or put my pen to work.

We cover the earth!

IDENTITY SERIES - CODE 1

MIRROR 10.4
A Living Reality Within The Believer

The New Testament is the indwelling reality of God in a man. It is an operation of life in the order of the life-giving spirit within a man. When you hear "The New Testament" what comes to your mind? Is it a set of books after Malachi? No sir! From Mathew to revelation is not the New Testament either. They are books that explain the New Testament. Most especially the Pauline epistles.

Question!

What Is The New Testament?

Answer!

The New Testament is a living reality in a person. It is the covenant between God and Christ as a living reality within the believer, currently being written in our heart.

And the entire books of the Bible captures the conception; the process and the consummation of the New Testament; WHICH IS GOD INDWELLING OF MAN IN HIS FULLNESS.

> "This is the covenant that I will make with them after those days, saith the Lord, I will put my laws into their hearts, and in their minds will I write them" Hebrews 10:16.

MIRROR TEN

This covenant is between God and Christ, and the result of this covenant is what we became in our spirit's nature; the believer's spirit personality (eternal life) is the blessing of this covenant between God and Christ. The believer is not the one in covenant with God. It is the Christ as the mediator. God is not in covenant with anyone apart from the man Christ, the mediator. We are the recipient of the blessings of the covenant.

This is why there are no conditions for you in Christ in other to receive God's blessings. As far as that thing is called a blessing from God, there is no condition attached to it. Your personal obedience is not what merits you for God's blessing. God has no blessing reserve for your obedience. God has blessed you already with ALL HIS blessing contained in eternal life in Christ.

Under the Old Covenant, the basis upon which the people receives God's blessing is their obedience.

> *"Now, therefore, if ye will OBEY my voice indeed, and KEEP my covenant, then ye shall be a PECULIAR TREASURE unto me above all people: for all the earth is mine; And ye shall be unto me a kingdom of priests and an holy nation. These are the words which thou shalt speak unto the children of Israel" Exodus 19:5-6.*

Unfortunately, they disobeyed. But the tide changed under the new covenant. The one who obeyed and forever kept the covenant in His blood is Christ. You are not the one to keep the covenant. In fact, to be sincere with you, you are not the one to "obey" the voice of God in a sense, that voice is what you became in your spirit's personality. The voice of God is that which He had spoken or came into being in the Son in redemption.

His present speaking is based on that voice. So, when you say God spoke to you or you heard the voice of God, it is actually the biding or the outflow of life from within your being. God is ever talking to you and forever will be.

This is why not yielding your soul to the leading of God is to deny yourself of that very thing that makes you who you are. So obeying the voice of the Lord for us is yielding to the knowledge of who we are from within. Any speaking that contradicts the nature of your spirit's personality is not of God. When God speaks, who you are is revealed, which is the personality of Christ.

> **Now it is on that ground of Christ's obedience we became the recipient of the blessing. This is why Peter could say this. "But ye are a chosen generation, a royal priesthood, a holy nation, a peculiar people; that ye should shew forth the praises of him who hath called you out of darkness into his marvellous light" 1 Peter 2:9.**

You can clearly see that wasn't based on your obeying to is His voice.

We go about demonstrating the goodness of God. You are not the disadvantaged at all never allow that cross your mind. The only problem is the lack of revelation knowledge, which produces the faith to enjoy that which you already have in Christ. Go for revelation knowledge at all cost.

MIRROR TEN

"Grace and peace be multiplied unto you through the KNOWLEDGE of God, and of Jesus our Lord, According as his divine power hath GIVEN unto us ALL THINGS that pertain unto life and godliness, through the KNOWLEDGE of him that hath called us to glory and virtue" 2 Peter 1:2-3.

"Blessed be the God and Father of our Lord Jesus Christ, who hath BLESSED us with ALL spiritual blessings in heavenly places in Christ" Ephesians 1:3.

God is no longer "Blessing" anyone again. Anything you come into is because you took advantage of the blessing, which is already yours in Christ. Don't believe the lies that God has blessed some more than others or God favours some more than others.

You can produce the same result any man has, with the given revelation knowledge. The difference is understanding. It has nothing to do with God. Your spirit's personality in Christ is the embodiment of all the blessings of God within and outside of eternity. These are contained in eternal life, which you became as the reality of the New Testament.

Go and study the New Testament, by that I mean go and do research and know who you are in Christ.

We are covering the earth!

IDENTITY SERIES - CODE 1

MIRROR 10.5

Understanding The Impact Of Spiritual Songs

The believer is an eternal fragrance unto the Lord. His sound is an eternal melody resonating in the heart of God the Father.

What Are Spiritual Songs?

Spiritual songs are the reality of revealed truth manifesting in the heart, which captures your spirit's personality as righteousness. It is teaching and speaking to ourselves the song the Lord sang to us in redemption. The Lord receives worship when we see ourselves in the light of the truth of what he has done in redemption (this is the song of the lord).

Redemption is an intoxicating wine the Father served us in Christ. You are not a drunkard if you don't understand the truth, and you cannot be drunk when you have the understanding. If you are drunk without an understanding, it is emotionalism.

Spiritual songs come as speaking or as a teaching or admonition.

> *"SPEAKING TO YOURSELVES in psalms and hymns and spiritual songs, singing and making melody IN YOUR HEART to the Lord"*
> *Ephesians 5:19.*

> *"Let the word of Christ dwell in you richly in all wisdom; TEACHING and[kai] ADMONISHING ONE ANOTHER in psalms and hymns and spiritual songs, SINGING with grace IN YOUR HEARTS to the Lord"* Colossians 3:16.

Note that the singing takes place in the heart. Spiritual songs coming forth as speaking is prophecy. This prophecy is not "foretelling" it is "forthtelling" or the calling forth of Christ from within us. That's why He said "speaking to yourselves" this is how major download of truth opens up in our midst as saints.

This is captured in Malachi 3:16.

> *"Then they that feared the Lord spake often one to another: and the Lord hearkened, and heard it, and a book of remembrance was written before him for them that feared the Lord, and that thought upon his name"* Malachi 3:16 (KJV).

Spiritual song coming forth as teaching is a reprove or admonition. It is an exposure of the believer's soul to the light of the truth of his spirit's personality.

The Lord's reproving a believer is a song in the believer's heart. There is absolutely no sense of unworthiness, fear or condemnation. If there is, then it is not the Lord!

The impact of spiritual songs both as speaking and teaching in our hearts is actually the singing to the Lord. What is coming to you right now is a spiritual song to your heart that resonates (sound) as singing to the Lord.

Understand that singing or worship is not in the words. The words are expressions of the song or the worship that has taken place in the heart. That is why even without words the believer is always in a constant flow of worship because of the revelation knowledge of the testimony of life within his heart.

This is what Paul captured as a spiritual song. It is that which manifests in the heart, concerning the testament of truth within our being. The singing is a heart to heart intercourse on the basis of divine revelation.

With God, singing is not a talent; otherwise, those verses above wouldn't apply to every believer, either is it a special ministry of some. Singing according to how Paul captured it by the spirit is how the believer ministers to the Lord within his heart.

So singing according to the Lord is not how sweet your "voice" sounds it is the resonance of the truth of the testimony of life within your heart.

So when spiritual songs come either as speaking or as teaching through anyone among us it facilitates the ministering or singing in the heart to the Lord!

Indeed worship is the truth of your identity manifest in the heart.

I call you blessed!

God bless you.

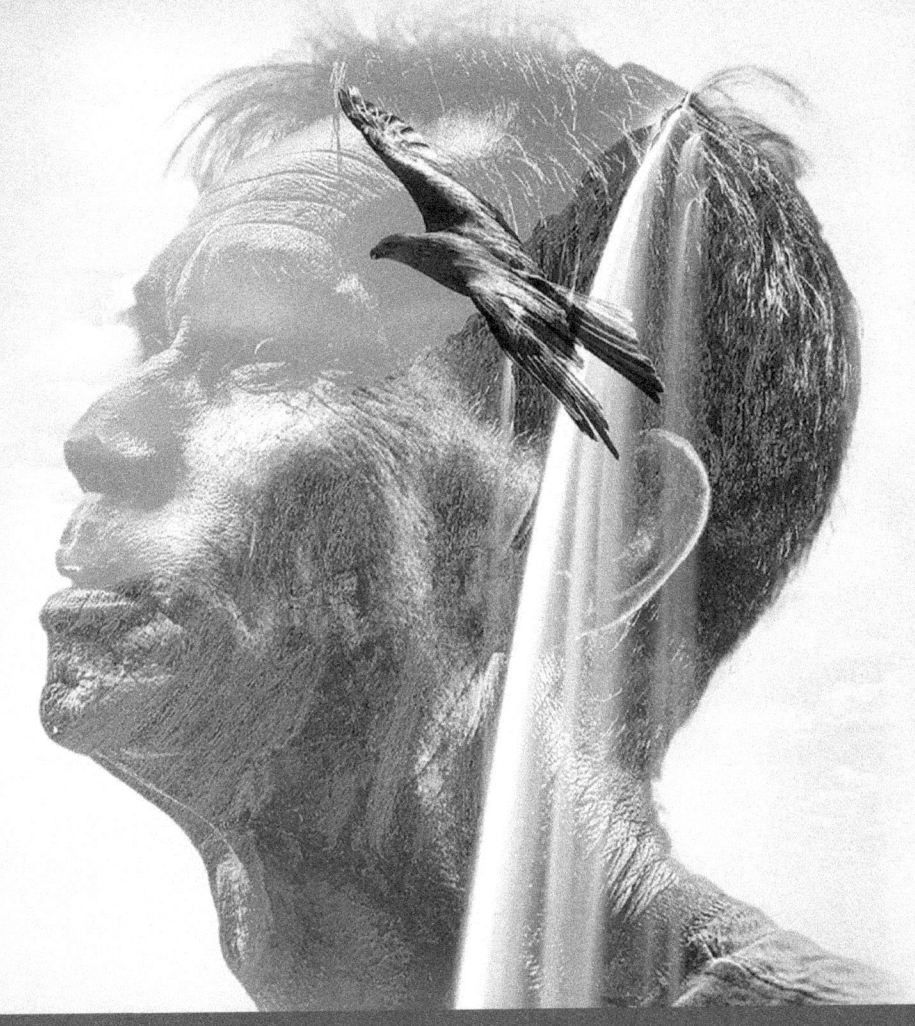

BLURB
TEACHING SERIES

IDENTITY SCHOOL OF REDEMPTION

IDENTITY SERIES - CODE 1

BLURB

Over the years, the Body of Christ has suffered as a result of the distorted identity of our spirit's nature in Christ. The consequences of this identity crisis resulted in a gross misrepresentation of Christ to the world. There is an urgency for the manifestation of the sons of God in our time.

Therefore, understanding that as believers, we have become one substance with the immortal Christ is crucial, and walking in the revelation knowledge of our spirit's nature as a quickening spirit helps us to function as life givers in this dying world.

This book therefore is written with one purpose in mind; to bring believers to encounter the immortal life of God in our spirit's nature in Christ. As you read, I encourage you to allow the Holy Spirit to bring you into this experience of immortality. Thus we are complete in the immortal Christ.

OTHER BOOKS

OTHER BOOKS BY
Saint Omo

Having read this book IDENTITY SERIES – CODE 1, written with great passion and candour, I am persuaded that the consciousness of the immortal life of God in your spirit has been wakened to explore the deeper dimensions of your spirit's identity in Christ.

Dear believer, you have the privilege also to get copies of Saint Omo's subsequent books written with depths of revelation and spiritual accuracy. The books would be in circulation shortly, both in print, eBooks and Kindle version on Amazon.com. Please watch out for these books to get copies for yourself, friends, colleagues, and families.

1. Identity Series – Code 2
2. Identity Series – Code 3
3. The Fellowship Of Gods
4. The Fatherhood Of God
5. Beyond The Fallen World
6. Basic Kingdom Practice (Making Spiritual Progress)
7. Understanding Redemption – Volumes 1 & 2

IDENTITY SERIES - CODE 1

www.ingramcontent.com/pod-product-compliance
Lightning Source LLC
Chambersburg PA
CBHW020930090426
42736CB00010B/1096